HOME FRONT
WICKHAM

For CLG, HMR, CNOR & DN

Crumps Barn Studio
Syde, Cheltenham GL53 9PN
www.crumpsbarnstudio.co.uk

Copyright © David Warwick 2024

Cover design & Map of Wickham in 1939 by Lorna Gray
Front cover: Photograph of marking out the Square ready for troops and vehicles
prior to D-Day, with air raid shelter and Wentworth House © The Stan Woodford
Collection, courtesy of Wickham Parish Council;
Back cover: Home Guard marching past church, *c.* 1943 © The Stan Woodford
Collection, courtesy of Wickham Parish Council; Photographs of Mrs D. A.
Warwick (née Bennett) *c.* 1920, and the author aged two © the author

All photographs © the author unless otherwise specified
Line drawings by Richard Bradley

All our books are printed on responsibly sourced paper from managed woodlands.
Printed in the UK by CMP, Poole.

ISBN 978-1-915067-46-3

HOME FRONT WICKHAM

DAVID WARWICK

*As a nation prepares for the Second World War,
Wentworth House opens its doors …*

Crumps Barn Studio

The family, that dear octopus from whose tentacles we never quite escape, nor in our innermost hearts ever quite wish to.

Dodie Smith – *Dear Octopus,* 1938

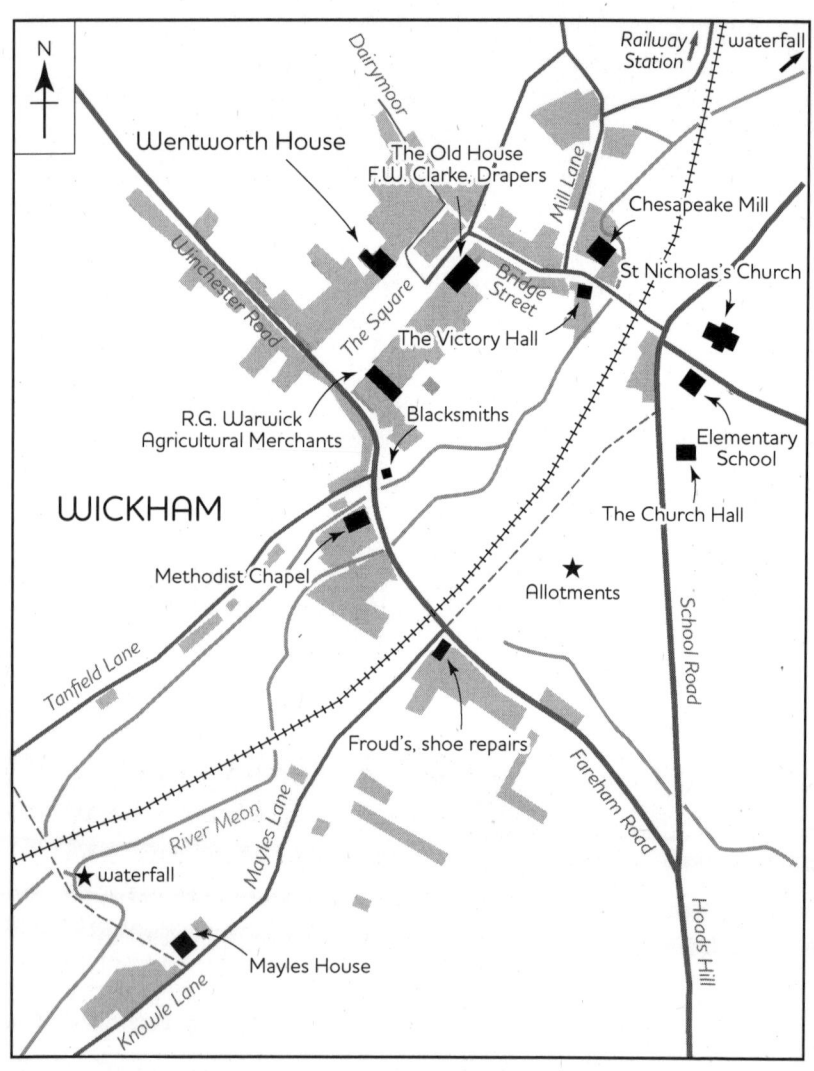

Map of Wickham in 1939 (not to scale)

INTRODUCTION

HOME FRONT WICKHAM is based on three sources. First, diaries kept almost continuously by my mother from 1939 to 1978, more particularly the early years when she was billeting officer for the area and first lady member of the Rural District Council. These journals from a wartime village, written in secret at a time when invasion was imminent, the outcome unknown, yet not discovered till the house clearance after her death, have direct first-hand immediacy. In contrast, there are the articles she wrote in the post-war years, knowing how the conflict had ended and the ways life had changed since then; more reflective in content. I brought a number of these together in two publications after her death as *Meon Valley Memories* and *Bygone Wickham*. Most of the direct quotations in this book are taken from this source.

Finally, I've incorporated my personal memories, light-hearted and anecdotal, brought to mind by events touched upon in the diaries. These bring out the individual personalities of those involved together with the everyday interplay of family life. We shared our home with ever-changing groups of evacuees who were welcomed to Wentworth to the accompaniment of eerie wailing sirens and the continual drone of planes – hostile and friendly – overhead. There were nights spent on camp beds down in the cellar or air raid shelter, blackout, tin hats, gas masks and the sound of distant gunfire. None of which seemed in any way unusual. It was what growing up must be like. I knew no other.

These three perspectives combine to determine the shape of the narrative. Without them I might not have fully appreciated the impact the war had on each one of us. It receives less direct mention in the diaries than I had anticipated. Specific events are recorded throughout, though not always those that might have been expected; the conflict is seldom commented upon yet it remains forever louring in the background, modifying and developing the personalities with which we had been born, myself included.

David Warwick

My mother Dorothy Alice Warwick (née Bennett) was the author of many diaries and articles, photograph c. 1920

The "wonderful clock", a large regulator clock bearing the Bennett name has been in the family c. 180 years (courtesy of Nichola King)

CHAPTER ONE

BACKGROUND

MY FATHER'S SIDE of the family were well-established in south Hampshire. Mother, Dorothy Alice Bennett, was a northerner, born at Grafton Street, Fishergate Hill, Preston, on 19 May 1894. Or 18th to be precise. When I came into the world on the very same date forty-two years later, she felt it a shame I should not have the day to myself, so we began celebrating her birthday on the 18th. This seems to have entered into the records, causing some confusion over the years. She was the second of four children: her sisters Eva and May were both living at the time she came south, but a brother, Richard, named after their father, died at an early age in 1904.

The family ran a jewellery and clockmaking business, established by Thomas Bennett at 21–23 Lune Street in 1848. It was handed over to his son, another Thomas, – my grandfather – whose ill-heath brought it to a close in 1926. He died on a visit to Wickham and is buried in the churchyard. A large regulator clock bearing the Bennett name has been in the family's possession for some 180 years. Mother trained as a teacher at *Whitelands* College, Putney, and as a pupil-teacher at Deepdale School, Preston, where she took up her first regular appointment. By now the first World War had broken out, particularly tragic for Preston as most of the young men – the *Preston Pals* – signed up, only to be slaughtered at Ypres.

My great-grandfather, the clockmaker Thomas Bennett,
c. 1870 (courtesy of Nichola King)

Meanwhile, at the other end of the country, their cousins – the Birchalls – owned a chemist shop in the Hampshire village of Wickham, some ten miles north of Portsmouth.

The population of the village would then have amounted to no more than 2000 but the square is one of the largest of its kind in the country. The Birchall shop stood, as it does today, in the southerly corner. The Birchalls were friendly with a nearby family, the Warwicks, whose mother had been widowed at the age of twenty-four leaving a couple of small sons; William was then two, and Reginald only nine months old. She became a dressmaker, recruiting six apprentices, her boys walking the three miles to Fareham and back each day for their schooling. William (W.A.G Warwick) became a well-known market gardener. Reginald planned to join his uncle, a merchant in London, but war was declared, he signed up and was sent for military training at Fulwood Barracks, Preston. Before he left, though, the Birchalls gave him the Bennetts' address, which was how my parents met.

Father never enjoyed good health. He developed tuberculosis and spent some time in hospital, reaching the rank of sergeant in the pay-corps before receiving his medical discharge. The couple married and returned to Wickham, which Mother was to describe.

[It was] a fairy-tale village, outwardly picturesque, with old-world charm, but without street lights, main water, gas or electricity, or any means of transport except two trains daily to London, no cooking facilities except oil stoves and coal and – worst of all – no sanitation. I had to pump the water I required from an old-fashioned pump which had a handle heavy to lift, held together by a leather band which occasionally broke and had to be replaced. This caused the water to taste of leather for several days. To have a bath was a major operation. I remember with horror the large tin tub, shaped like a coffin which took ages to fill. Each kettle of water had to be separately heated and the first was always cold before the second was added. It took the whole evening to get an uncomfortable bath. My cooking had to be done by oil. I used a stove called 'Perfection', but it did not live up to its name. It is, however, astonishing what one can get used to and after much experimentation I became quite a successful cook.[1]

My father, R.G. Warwick, Sgt, pay-corps, 1915

---

[1] Warwick, D.A., 1982, pp 6—7

My parents opened a small hardware store next to Birchall's where, living in such conditions in the tiny rooms above the shop, my sister, Mary, and brother, Brian (Reginald Brian Bennett), were born. And, if this were not enough, shortly after their arrival in Wickham, in the absence of a headmaster, Mother was asked to help out at the village school. At that time, this was a Victorian building adjacent the church. Several candidates had applied for the post but, following an initial visit, disappeared, never to be seen again! This was a very different proposition from her experience at Deepdale, which had been modern, up-to-date, with all the latest equipment. Looking back, she was to remember:

> There were about 180 children on roll, the long classroom partitioned so it could be divided into two. There was one more classroom, making three in all … Heating consisted of a large open fire which kept those sitting in front of it warm, but those at the back frozen. The other two rooms had a circular coke stove though which gave out acrid fumes, requiring constant attention. The long wooden forms had no support for the children's backs and there seemed to be a total lack of apparatus of any kind … My one helper was Phoebe Fridle, a girl of fifteen, the "monitor", who did her best to cope with the eight and nine-year-olds whilst I took all the rest in a large room with the partition pulled back.

> Many of the children came from very poor families, some having to be provided with boots from

charity. Without these they would have had to walk barefoot on rough roads for long distances. There was no means of transport and the school took in many children from North Boarhunt, Kingsmead and Mislingford. During the wet cold winter they arrived tired out. Attendance was very erratic for, during the potato harvest, the children were kept home to help out. In the fruit season they were kept absent and harvest time was exceptionally busy for them. Because of this, school holidays were arranged to fit in with these special occasions … The children had a certain amount of farm work to do before they came to school. They had to feed animals, take round milk or do some of the housework.[2]

The annual award of boots from Clark's drapers for the three best attenders must have been most welcome. Another prize was a banner, bestowed each year by the church to the best of the seventeen village schools in the area for spiritual knowledge and practice. To Mother's delight, under her tutelage Wickham came out on top, the managers awarding them a day's holiday.

Another inspection was not nearly as welcome:

Some of the children were verminous and had to be excluded until it was safe to readmit them. They were sent home with a pink card giving their parents a maximum of two weeks in which to deal with the matter. When the child returned to school a green

---

[2]   Ibid, pp 18—19

card had to be returned, signed by the district nurse certifying that all was well.

The appointed school doctor used to pay an annual visit by horse and trap accompanied by a nurse. Each child was examined behind a screen in the largest classroom. It was on one of these occasions that for the first time I saw body lice. I think that this was the most disagreeable experience I had in the whole of my teaching life.[3]

The stress of this alongside bringing up the family under spartan conditions affected Mother's health. The doctor advised moving to higher ground where they would not be on top of the business. Hoad's Hill seemed perfect and in six weeks the Knight brothers, Harold and Monty, the local builders completed their new home, *Preston Ridge*. Here it was that my brother, Richard (Richard George), was born.

Finally, in 1930 the family moved to *Wentworth,* a large three-story Georgian house dating from 1775 on the northerly side of the Square. A glimpse of the property as it was in the 1920s – the building, garden, beyond this a smaller cottage, and between them a stream – is provided by A.V. Barber, who stayed there with her uncle as a ten-year-old. The accompanying sketches show Wentworth, both inside and out, together with the village as it then was.[4] She tells, for example of a conflagration breaking out two doors down at the *Kings Head*. The fire engine that got its water from the

---

[3] Op cit, 19
[4] Barber, A.V., Days at Wickham, 1966

river took three quarters of an hour to arrive, and then one of the hoses burst, soaking onlookers. Meanwhile, flames had spread along next door's creeper, the old lady who live there carrying her valuable paintings out into the garden to save them. Next morning the hotel was *"black, broken and sad."*[5]

By the time the Warwicks arrived the house was in a dilapidated condition, having survived not only fire but flood. The stream at the top of the garden had overflowed, a regular occurrence apparently, this time discharging currents of water along gravel paths down through the house. *Harrods Estates* had the property on their books for over a year before local builders the Knight brothers, whose premises were next door, set about the renovations, scraping away the mud and debris, and re-painting the sage-green interior ivory.

Here it was, at 4:10 on the afternoon of 19 May 1936 that I was born. My name – David William – was suggested by Mrs Kinnear, the doctor's wife. Twenty-five years later it was their son – Jimmy Kinnear – who was to bring my own elder child into the world.

5 Ibid, 54

Father with Brian, Dick, and Mary, c. 1930

Wentworth House, the Square, Wickham

CHAPTER TWO

THE HOUSE WHERE I WAS BORN

I WAS BAPTIZED at St Nicholas' Church on 22 June. The godparents were my sister Mary, Mr A.E. Roberts, who was to play such a major role in the village during the war and the years that followed, and Father's brother, Uncle Will.

It was at Wentworth that I was to spend the first twenty-six years of my life, and the house looks much the same now as it did then: shuttered windows, spiked iron railings, worn stone steps that led up to the front door with a brass knocker and letter box, the façade swathed top to bottom in rich red creeper glowing gloriously in the autumn sunshine. The interior, though, has changed considerably over the years.

The entrance hall led into three large ground floor rooms. To the front, its windows facing onto the Square, was the *Dining Room,* so-called as we ate there when the whole family were at home. To the centre was a large multi-leaved table; at one side stood a glass-fronted cupboard displaying the best of the china and silverware. Bookcases – constructed specially by the Knight brothers – stretched end-to-end along the other, topped with the fully-rigged model of a galleon under full sail.

In reality it was an all-purpose room where we spent most of our time, playing card or board games at the table, with marbles or soldiers on the carpet, reading books or listening to the radio around the fire which was kept alight most of the year. Mother was very proud of the new surround consisting of stones of all shapes and sizes, but it took several years of regular polishing before their real colours were revealed.

Behind the chimney, a little way up, was a flue which could be opened and closed manually diverting some of the heat to a tank to provide us with hot water. A visit from the sweep was a great occasion. Furniture would be cleared from the room or covered with dust sheets. The first of a series of flexible wooden rods with a brush attached would be shoved up through the fireplace. The rest were progressively screwed together and pushed further dislodging soot as they went until – great excitement to see who would be the first to spot it – the brush shot out of the chimney at the top. It would then be withdrawn bringing the remaining soot with it.

To the back of the house the *Drawing Room* had floor-to-ceiling windows leading out into the garden. Kept in pristine condition and used for special occasions only, it was comfortably furnished with easy chairs and a grand piano. Here Mother kept a steadily-mounting collection of teapots and there were two shoulder-high Chinese vases into which any number of toys or pieces of rubbish were surreptitiously dropped over the years. Between these two rooms was a doorway, kept permanently locked, behind which a staircase led down to the cellar; dank, dark, cobwebbed, somewhat of a mysterious domain used primarily for the storage of coal, delivered via a narrow chute from a manhole in the square.

Alongside the Drawing Room, also leading out into the garden, was a side room used in those days for jam-making, the preserving and bottling of fruit, stuffing of poultry, etc. Its main feature was a large French dresser on which plates of all sizes were displayed. At a later date, with the installation of an Aga, we took most of our meals in this room.

Jutting out from the back of the house was a scullery and two additional rooms, once the servants' quarters, reached via a passage with a series of delicately-strung bells plus an indicator showing which of the various rooms in the main house had summoned attention. I remember it being still in use for entertainment purposes as a child. This part of the house was rented out in the immediate post-war years.

The second floor consisted of two large bedrooms, with my parents' directly above the Dining Room, memorable not only for a gigantic double bed but two hideous statuettes of Joseph and Mary each protected by a glass dome and a cupboard used in days past as a closet for ladies to powder their wigs.[6] Alongside was the bathroom, facing out onto the Square, and the toilet; old-fashioned, with a long dangling chain. When tugged it discharged torrents of water gushing down into the bowl, and took ages to refill. Far more exciting this for a three to four-year-old than the modern push-button type. As were the toilet rolls. These were thin, transparent, unpleasantly germicidal, and almost non-absorbent. Wonderful as tracing-paper, though. Best of all, hidden

---

[6]   op cit, 36

between individual sheets were colourful nursery rhymes such as *Little Bo Peep, Jack & Jill,* etc, rewritten to encourage frugality and boost the wartime anti-waste drive – brilliant as a device for selling the product; disastrous regarding the overall economic concept considering the rapidity I got through that toilet paper to reach the stories.

To the back of the house, my brothers shared one of two rooms overlooking the garden. The other – where I had been born – was cut off from the rest of the house when the property was divided after the war. There were three rooms on the top floor, two overlooking the Square, known as *Mary's* and *David's,* with an attic or box room facing the garden at the rear.

Mary with Dick and Brian, c. 1937

THE GARDEN STRETCHED behind Wentworth – a long narrow lawn, a line of pear trees and three poplars, then hardly reaching the height of the house, later to tower above it with enormous roots heaving out in all directions. Now all gone. Gravel paths led past fruit trees and vegetable patches up to the Studio, a single-story building with a large skylight designed specifically for an artist. This probably dates from the early 1920s when the artist Evelyn Woodroffe Hicks was in residence. Barber recalls her uncle using it as a carpentry workshop with red brick flooring; her sketch shows it strewn with his tools. Apparently it was later commandeered by the army for the detention of disorderly troops, who were subsequently expelled by Mother for use as a school. Beside the Studio stood a barn, used as a storeroom, and beside this, the tallest and most terrifying swing I've ever encountered. A homemade affair, the seat was attached to a couple of ropes dangling from the highest branch of a nearby tree. Once it had gained full momentum, you were swung at enormous speed up into the uppermost foliage, then down in a perilous arc, backwards and forwards clinging on for dear life.

The studio was separated from the rest of the property by a small wall and the stream that had caused so many floods prior to restoration. Along our side of the wall grew three peach trees, my sister's pride and joy; woe betide anyone that went near them. Similarly the greenhouse, where Father lovingly tended his grapes. Alongside the greenhouse were hutches in which my brothers kept their rabbits – until an invasion of rats from the stream slaughtered the lot. I suppose in a large family such as ours, each needed to mark out their own territories. Behind the Studio lay Blackman's Field, the home of several cows and numerous cowpats. Knights' premises stretched the full length of our garden on the one side, to the other lived Mrs Bruce, our childhood adversary. Toys, model airplanes and balls of all kinds found their way over the wall into her property, requests for their return, however polite, being promptly rejected. This resulted in a series of escapades in which I was perched on the top of the wall to keep lookout whilst one of my brothers clambered over it and began a feverish search whilst the other shouted instructions as where best to look.

My earliest experiences were bounded within these two walls: the Knight brothers' business to one side, Mrs Bruce to the other; between the spiked metal fence at the front of the house, the stream flowing past the end of the garden at the rear. From my bedroom window, though, was a wider world promising even greater adventures which I was eager to explore.

Grandfather and Grandmother Bennett with Brian in Wentworth
garden, c.1930 with pear trees and the studio beyond

Bridge Street, Wickham, with village dip-hole in foreground

CHAPTER THREE

PRAMBULATIONS

BEYOND WENTWORTH THE countryside was virtually free of traffic, abounding in wildlife. Red squirrels could be seen along the Winchester Road and windscreen washers were in constant use on car journeys to keep them free from insects. I'd wake each summer's morning to a solid wall of birdsong from all sides; the clatter of pony's hooves as our milk was delivered by the one-handed man from Parret's dairy. The blacksmith's clash of metal on anvil could be heard throughout the year, as could the whistle of the steam train running along the Meon Valley Line from Fareham to Alton; then all-change for London.

I recall being wheeled around the village in a large well-sprung pram; this must have been from 1939 to the early 40s. En route, we'd pass various landmarks with mother telling me tales relating to each – captivating, whilst at the same time providing a primitive kind of socialization. Over the years to come, certain values would continually be stressed in these stories. Role models abounded, both positive and negative, ensuring I was aware of how to behave and something of the community I was about to join.[7]

The 'prambulation' began almost as soon as we left the house. Tunnels were said to run beneath the square along which smugglers – known locally as 'owlers' – used to bring their contraband from the river to the *King's Head*. Similarly, getaway passages were believed to exist for poachers evading the law with entrances at the Old House (Doctors Hole) and Tanfield Lane (Crook's Hole). Dire consequences awaited those who are caught. The smugglers in particular, who would be hung in chains at Portsmouth dockyard to be eaten by crabs – I think I must have been spared the gory details at the time – until three tides had washed over them. Search as I could, I never did find evidence to verify such tales.

Directly opposite Wentworth was West's butchers. The founder, Walter West, town crier in Victorian times, had been given the nickname of Birdie on account of his high-pitched, squeaky voice. "If each before their own door sweep," he'd declare night and morning along with local news and announcements, "the village will be clean." The inference – toys to be cleared away, bedrooms left tidy – made clear.

Next door, the Old House, had been the home of the notorious Baxter who'd upset the villagers in a number of ways, most notably by living openly with his mistress (once more I'd have been spared the particulars). Taking the law into their own hands, they declared a 'Skimmington', banging pots and pans night and day outside the residence ("And let that be a lesson to you!").

---

[7] The historic background to most of these sites can be found in the Local History Society's *Guide to Historic Wickham*

Alongside the Old House, at the juncture of the Square and Bridge Street stood a drapery established by F.W. Clarke in the 1890s. He'd been a flautist who'd played not only with Paganini but at Buckingham Palace. Whilst in India he'd brought a charging bull to a standstill with nothing more than a stare. Better still, he'd installed a kind of miniature railway system or overhead cash-carrier connecting various departments – men's, women's, children's, finance, management, etc – one with the other. You'd pay for your purchase, the money would be placed in a small container and sent catapulting across to finance; a receipt would be written, this and any change placed in the container and whizzed back to the shop floor, by which time the goods had been wrapped. Inter-departmental messages or queries could be dispatched throughout the large two-storey building, saving time, eliminating mistakes and avoiding fraud. I saw precisely the same system, operating in Russia in the late 1990s.

Bridge Street winds down a steep hill at the bottom of which it crosses the river Meon. Chesapeake Mill, built from the timbers of a ship captured during the American Civil War[8], has long been a tourist attraction. Opposite stands Victory Hall, formerly a brewery, now a community centre, but mother was always far more interested in the dip-hole from which villagers used to draw water. A small child had lost their footing on the steps that led down to it and (cue another cautionary tale) was only found weeks later washed out to sea.

Mother waxed even more lyrical about the Jutes, fierce

---

[8] Warwick, 1983, pp 27—9

warriors who'd arrived in this country alongside the Angles and Saxons after the end of Roman rule. Some landed in Kent. Others sailed further along the coast, into Southampton Water before making landfall at just this spot and creating the settlement later known as Wickham. Their descendants were a set apart, unique throughout the country. Quite different from any other boy or girl she'd taught, so Mother maintained; you could spot them a mile off.

Chesapeake Mill, Wickham

"Economic in their style of speech," affirmed a later commentator. "Curious, both in looks and manner, quite different from us true-blue Hampshire."[9]

Be this as it may, the Jutes were far more to my liking than

9   Jones, S.R., *England South,* London, Studio Publications, 1948, 128

what I've heard so far. One couldn't imagine them sweeping their doorsteps, tidying away their toys at night; continually being wary of slippery surfaces when out walking.

By now we'd have reached St Nicholas' church, standing on the crossroads at the end of Bridge Street. Several stories relating to it then persisted in living memory. Mr Stich, for example, once employed by the Italian Ambassador at the Court of St James, used to drive – in full regalia – the Lord of the Manor to church each Sunday in a coach-and-four together with outriders. He'd been held in almost as much awe as his master. Part of Wickham's folk history relates to St Nicholas' bells. Seven of these had been ordered from the foundry in Victorian times but the external measurements of the tower had been mistaken for those of the interior and so one of them would not fit. It was left standing outside the building for several months whilst the parish council considered what should be done till one night it was spirited away.

As I grew up we sometimes visited the churchyard to replenish the flowers at grandmother's grave. This stood halfway down the path quite a distance from the building. I remember being sent back to fill the watering can, making my terrified way there and back between the tombstones. Occasionally I'd be taken into the church where I was allowed to activate the bellows of the disused old manually-operated organ.

The other main interest was (and still is) the Uvedale Memorial. Constructed of alabaster and marble it dates back to the 16th century and depicts the knight in full armour alongside his wife, below which are kneeling statuettes of their eight children, three sons and five daughters. There is also a ninth, holding a skull, signifying that they died at an early age. At the time of the Civil War, the building was ransacked by the parliamentarians, who were said to have pitched a statue of St Anthony into the nearby river. In my time the knight's helmet stood on top of the memorial. That was before the powers that be removed it to Winchester Museum for safekeeping. Maybe they had long memories?

Turning right at the church, along School Road, we'd take a short-cut through the allotments, parallel to the railway line (now Wykeham Field).[10] This brought us out beneath the bridge which crosses Fareham Road. On the opposite side stood Mr Froud's tiny shop where we took our shoes to be repaired. Continuing up Mayles Lane, we'd reach an imposing old building, Mayles House, set back from the road on the right. Here we'd pause to read an inscription on the gate: *Manners Maketh Man*, the motto of William of Wykeham[11] the celebrated 14th century Chancellor of England, who'd been born in the village. "Everything was done by him", it was said, "nothing without him was done." As a child he'd mixed well with others, played football with them, taken part in archery contests in the Square and loved animals – squirrels, bees, pigeons, even bears! All drummed into us from infancy. And epitomized in that three-word motto. Unfortunately, it lost everything in the translation. "Manners" as my Latin teacher later explained, derives from "mores", meaning "custom".

---

[10] The route of this footpath is marked with a dashed line on *Map of Wickham in 1939*, see Introduction

[11] For best local account, see Retallick

Cutting through the fields behind Mayles House was a little-known pathway. Here water cascaded continually over a small weir where the river had been dammed, to my mind one of the village's two waterfalls. The second, very similar, is to be found to the north of the village halfway down Swales Lane. The pathway took us along the back of someone's garden out into Tanfield Lane. This led down to the Square past the old Methodist Chapel on the right, in those days the blacksmith's. We'd cringe in the doorway as horses of gigantic stature were backed into the tiny premises taking up most of the space available. Hand-operated bellows coaxed the furnace to face-blistering heat, a metal horseshoe would be reached down, measured for size and thrust into the coals. Hammered into shape and doused with a sizzle and clouds of steam, it was nailed – painlessly we were assured – onto the hoof and pared into shape with a sharp knife. Since then the building has been put to a variety of uses.

The new chapel stood, as it does now, on the other side of the road, although – like the blacksmith's – subsequently used for different purposes. A little further down was the wonderful weathervane that used to stand on top of Wheatley's yard. This consisted of a series of tiny figures each performing a specific task. As the wind blew, one of them would be actually sawing wood, another hammering in nails, a third using an adze and so on.

An alternative route would take us up Winchester Road to the site of one of Wickham's old toll gates. This used to be manned by Harry Boyes and was the scene of many skirmishes between gangs from our village and those from Botley. It was also the source of one of Mother's favourite tales; "Hang him up and cut him down!" chanted our lads, a slogan dating back to the time just after public executions had been abolished. One of the spectators at the last such spectacle offered to demonstrate how it was done in the bar of the *Bugle Inn*. He'd just placed his head in the noose when a band passed by. Everyone rushed to the window, leaving him to choke to death. "Little hell" taunted Botley in response, referring to the legend that when God fashioned the world He had a little bit of earth left and didn't know what to do with it. So He created Wickham.

Another of the characters I learnt about on these walks was Neddy Molton, who owned Inglefield Farm, Soberton and had a reputation for being a bit of a tartar. His workers lived in residence having been hired for months at a time. Once he offered to lend some of them to a neighbour. Easily recognised, he told his friend, they were the ones without eyebrows – worn off from looking through the cracks in the barn to see if he was coming! One of them decided he'd had enough and did a moonlight flit. Before he went, though, he scratched on the tarred side of the barn:

> Neddy Molton, Inglefield Farm,
> Thatched cottage and tiled barn,
> Rusty Bacon and sour beer,
> And I'm not ****** well stopping here![12]

In rural, relatively isolated communities such as ours, where transport had always been limited, communication was via the spoken rather than the written word. One made

---

[12] Warwick, 1983, 37

one's own entertainment and stories such as these would have been very much a part of it. Tales such as those of Walter West and Harry Boyes, Neddy Molton, Messrs Baxter, Clarke, and Stich, set in their specific locations and handed down from generation to generation, formed an unwritten folk history. As such they served a social as well as a recreational purpose. But in a fast-moving, mobile society, as the landscape is transformed, the folk dispersed, who will be left to tell such tales?

My father, c. 1935

CHAPTER FOUR

THE PEACETIME YEARS

MOTHER WAS TO keep a twenty-six-page handwritten account of the first year of my life; she also sent off for a horoscope from one of the popular papers. This took the precise time and exact location of my birth, scanned the heavens to trace trajectories of various bodies, and came up with some twenty pages of fuzzily duplicated sheets; flattering, but contradictory in their advice. And in 1939 she began the first of the five-year diaries, in which she was briefly to record the happenings of the day.

The small portion of the diary relating to the pre-war months, portrays Wentworth as a flurry of activity. Both my parents were now into their mid-forties; 'Reg' and 'Dos' as affectionately they called one another. My sister was away in France, the only English student at a convent in Chartres, but my brothers had to be got off to boarding school – Brian to Oxford and Dick as chorister at Chichester Cathedral, where Brian later joined him at the Prebendal School. Both of them had their names down for Lancing College near the south coast, but with war imminent they ended up at Bloxham, near Banbury, where they'd be safe from bombs. I never heard Dick called by any other name – certainly never Richard – but when together he would refer to Brian as 'Joe'. Three times a year their clothes needed getting together, socks darned, nametags sewn on, along with trips to Southsea where additions to their uniforms could be purchased, followed by a session at *Handley's* for the infliction of the regulation haircut. Our reward: the largest of cream teas imaginable. Brian, at the age of ten, was the most outgoing of the lot of us, but never happy at leaving home. He was miserable each term as he left, resulting in general nervousness and minor afflictions such as styes. Dick remained cheerful enough although Christmas dinner for the family often had to take place before or after 25th December when he was involved in the Cathedral services.

Summer holidays were not much of a problem but open fires needed lighting to air the boys' bedrooms before term ended in the winter months – as they were whenever we had visitors. I remember both of them returning from Bloxham at Christmas and Easter suffering from chilblains which needed massaging with an ointment called *Snowfire*. With no central heating the downstairs fires were kept constantly alight throughout the latter part of the year. Coal would be delivered in large sacks from the station and shot via the chute into the cellar. From there it was brought up in buckets as and when required. The cold ashes needed raking out before a new fire was laid ready for lighting. This entailed a careful arrangement of newspaper and sticks and the use of a large pair of bellows kept in readiness alongside the Dining Room fireplace. On either side two ferocious-looking black metal Chinese cats stood on guard over various pokers and tongs leant up against their tails. Each had a ring in its mouth. If they wanted me out of the way, my brothers would sit me in front of them, remove the rings and say the cats would bite if I stirred.

The return of my brothers from school meant – so Mother records – three weeks of dirty washing. A constant supply of clean sheets was also required. Water from the tap was unsuitably hard so rainwater, collected from a large tank to the rear of the house, was used instead. Numerous journeys to and fro had to be made before a large porcelain sink in the back scullery was filled, the sheets soaked for some time in the greenish-coloured liquid before receiving a vigorous pummelling. They were then squeezed through the hand-operated mangle – up at Gravel Hill, Auntie Emma's seriously deformed thumb bore testimony to the dangers involved. Finally, pristine white, the sheets would be hoisted to the ceiling via a series of pulleys and left to dry on a large wooden rack.

Before the arrival of electricity Wentworth must have been almost completely self-sufficient. At the very back of the building stood the Engine Room; once the stables according to A.V. Barber, who remembers them being used to house a generator which made a good deal of noise; the home of some kind of a monster so she believed. Later it was converted for the storage of coal, but the remnants of disused machinery and some of the old bulbs remained on the upper floor in my time. Monsters of different kind as well. It was festooned with spider webs and I got into no end of trouble for locking one of my 'minders' in there. How was I to know she'd have hysterics?

By 1936, Wentworth had electricity on the national grid but was still self-sufficient in several other ways.

Besides cooking for the whole family, Mother spent entire afternoons in the autumn jam making – somewhat of a hit-or-miss process as she never quite knew whether or not it would set. Raspberries, gooseberries, blackcurrants and other soft fruit came from the garden; there was a regular supply of strawberries from Uncle Will's nursery at Gravel Hill, Shedfield, blackberry-picking expeditions in the woodlands along Knowle Lane, sometimes loganberries from Frith Farm, where my godfather, Mr Roberts, had pioneered their cultivation in this country. All of us would be involved in the preliminaries – peeling, stemming, top-and-tailing, etc., each requiring a specific skill – together with the writing and sticking-on of labels. Later the whole process was simplified enormously by the arrival of the Kilner jar.

Less of a spectator sport was preparing salt ready for every-day use. It arrived in large blocks which had to be broken down into brick-sized portions. The family, or whoever was available, would sit round the table which had been covered with sheets of newspaper rubbing two of the smaller blocks together to see who could produce the largest quantity of the kind of granulated salt we have today in the shortest time. Meat was to become a scarce commodity. Severely rationed in the years that followed, the greatest ingenuity was required if there was to be any variety in what we ate. Here the mincer came into its own, and I had great fun forcing the meat into a funnel at the top, turning the handle and watching it extruded in various shapes according to which of several interchangeable disks had been inserted. Oranges were even shorter in supply but a machine similar in size and operation shredded their skin for the preparation of marmalade.

All of this was recorded in passing through the pages of the diaries; sometimes in barely legible writing. As were the rituals of family life that were beginning to be established. Church-going was one of these. Father and Mother would often attend early morning Communion, but all of us were expected to join them at Mattins each Sunday when at home. The service, Mother remembers:

> Followed exactly the same one to which I had been accustomed and whole families attended regularly, sitting in the same rows each week. Many of the larger houses had pews reserved for them, the name of the house being shown on a tablet at its end. It was not until the 1930s that these were removed and everyone sat where they wished.[13]

All of us walked down together as a family to take our place for Morning Service, usually sitting halfway along the north transept. On one occasion, Dick was seized with a nosebleed and had to be laid down horizontally throughout the sermon. The rector must have thought he'd dozed off. Dinner would then be taken in the Dining Room, with Father ceremoniously sharpening the carving knife and then doing the honours.

Christmas is a special time with most families, although each have their own way of celebrating it. In ours the rituals had, for the most part, been established in the years before my birth. Long multi-coloured streamers, for instance, pre-war in origin and brought down from the attic, every year a

---

[13] Warwick, 1982, 37

little more faded. Indentations at the four corners of the dining room marked precisely where they were to be hung, in the selfsame position, well into the 1960s. Breakfast would be followed by the opening of presents in the Drawing Room from which we'd been excluded for several days. Now we'd find them laid out for us on separate chairs ready for us to open: the "ceremony of the presents" as Mother dubbed it. With so little available in the shops they were usually of a practical nature – a torch, penknife, socks, hankies, or handmade, alongside my *Rupert* annuals that is. Christmas cards were also designed together by the family; to be delivered next day at the cost of 1½d postage!

Another feature of the occasion was the Christmas pudding. This would have been prepared on the last Sunday before Advent, usually towards the end of November, when each of us helped stir the mixture in a large bowl.[14] There was always great excitement as it was served and we looked to see which of the silver farthings or tiny charms – horseshoes, wedding bells, shamrock, etc – added prior to cooking, was part of our helping. Father kept a supply of wines and spirits in a cupboard in the hall, but Christmas Day is the only occasion I can remember them being brought out. One year he decided to celebrate in style, consulted the gurus in the national press and ordered the bottle recommended for each course. I was too young to partake, but judging from the expression on everyone's face, the comments for months to come, it's hardly surprising that the experiment was never

---

[14] Based on the collect (prayer) set by the Anglican Church for that day: *Stir up, we beseech thee, O Lord, the wills of thy faithful people ...*

repeated. Quite often the family from Gravel Hill would come over in the afternoon, or vice-versa, when Father and Uncle Will would smoke cigars before we'd turn on the radio for the King's speech. All of us would stand for the National Anthem. The afternoon was usually spent in playing one of several board games.

ANOTHER REGULAR, LESS spiritual, occasion was Fareham market, where we had a stall, whilst birthdays – six of these altogether – became eagerly-anticipated staging-posts throughout the year. As at Christmas, gifts in those days tended to be handmade with specific individuals in mind. I remember especially the hours Dick spent preparing a toy sweetshop for me, together with my name above the window and tiny bottles of sweets on each of the shelves. Another year (my sixth) I'd been clamouring for a desk. My parents' response was to get the Knight brothers to make me one with a sloping lid, inkwells and a chair that fitted under it. Two years later it was a swing; not purchased from the shop but again constructed by the Knights and erected in the back garden. Not as exciting as the one I vaguely remember up at the Studio, but not a fraction as dangerous. And, throughout the war years, my Godfather, Mr Roberts, threw a birthday party for me in a genuine horse-drawn caravan at Frith farm.

BEYOND THE FOUR walls of Wentworth, Fair Day and Bonfire Night seem to have been the two great events in village life; the latter still is.

Wickham Pageant, 1938/9, Dick 7th from right, Brian 4th

Fair Day was held annually on or around 20th May, co-inciding precisely with my and Mother's birthdays. The tradition of damming the river that morning and sending any stranded fish up to the squire for his breakfast was, by 1939, a thing of the past. As was the notion that a frost on that day was the sign of a poor summer to come. The grown-ups remembered when children carrying flower-decked hoops would parade through the square, whilst in my time, remnants of the chains that closed Fareham Road to traffic on Fair Day could still be seen, fixed to the bridge by Wheatley's Yard. By then the cattle market had transferred to the fields at the bottom of Mill Lane, with horses being put through their paces up and down the Winchester Road. Following this one of the ponies would be taken into the *Star Inn* for a pint of beer. Meanwhile, the rest of the square had been taken over by the razzmatazz of the modern-day amusements with stalls and rides coming right up to the edge of our front door. 1939 was to be the last fair to be held in peacetime but, against all the odds, it returned the following year, reverting to the cattle market only in 1941 and 42. Things returned to normal in 1943, but it isn't mentioned in the diary for 1944, and in 1945 it had to be cancelled through foot-and-mouth disease.

5th November had always been a day for great celebration in the village. Most of them seem to have got out of hand. Best keep your houses locked and a careful watch over your gardens in the days leading up to it; furniture, branches of trees, logs, spare sleepers from the railway station – anything combustible – would be heaped in a great pile in the middle of the Square. Barrels filled with tar would be rolled out from their hiding-places, on one occasion a delivery wagon was stolen; all to be burnt on the great day. In my time things were more civilized. Even so, the bonfire was prepared weeks ahead, with families turfing out their old junk and the children scouring the countryside for anything inflammable. It often towered up to the height of our first-floor bedrooms with the fire brigade standing by. Until, that is, the telegraph wires that stretched across the Square melted and the celebrations were transferred to the recreation ground. This was a disappointment for the younger generation, one of whose sports was diablo, in which disc-like spools balanced on a string were tossed in the air – in this case the competition being to see who could get theirs highest over the wires.

A number of groups and social organizations flourished in the village, mostly for the distaff side of the family: Women's Institute, Mothers' Union, Over Sixty Club, etc., whilst for my father there was the Southampton branch of the *National Federation of Ironmongers.* His family were already well established in the community; not so my mother, who – coming from a busy northern town – was to take some time in settling down to village life.

Sketch of Wentworth House by Arthur Pitt

The shop still stands on the southerly side of the Square, pictured here in early 1930s. Father on left, now morphed into Warwick Lane

CHAPTER FIVE

HEART OF THE FAMILY

WICKHAM IN THE late 30s was a small close-knit community within which social divisions were clearly defined. A case, as Mother put it, of:

> everyone having his own place in society and keeping within that place. All were quite friendly. It was just that through long established custom each class remained within its own particular circle, and this worked well.[15]

This situation is implicit throughout all of the diaries, and it was hardly surprising that, shy and self-effacing as she was, it took some time for her to settle down.

Mother, though, was a person of boundless energy and an accomplished violin player. She'd been a member of an orchestra in Preston and taught the instrument when she came south. To her delight she discovered that Wickham had an orchestra of its own. This consisted of about thirty members, financed and run by Squire Long of Corhampton – rumour had it that he never employed anyone unless they could play

---

[15] Warwick, 1982, 9

a musical instrument or were willing to learn how to do so. It was conducted by the rector, Rev Hungerford Duke – who was also the cellist. Mr F.W. Clarke, whose expertise on the flute has already been noted, was also a member of the group. There seems to have been no end of musical talent in the village. Down at the school, Headmaster Billy Langford played the trombone.

"I can picture him now," Mother was to recall, "standing in the front of the class playing the instrument, nearly pushing the children off the back seats."

The orchestra rehearsed regularly and, in the months leading up to the war played at local fetes, open days, etc. sometimes accompanied by the Gosport Military Band. Back home Mother practiced as often as she could. Every so often one of the strings would break and I'd be sent to buy a new one at *Antrobuses* in Bridge Street. A scary expedition this. The shop was small and dark, its shelves decked with clocks of all shapes and sizes, each ticking away, liable to strike when least expected. Worse still, the proprietor would appear unexpectedly, wraith-like from the interior.

By 1939, though, Mother was well enough established to play an active part in the community. A member of the Parish Council together with a range of other village societies, she was the first woman elected to the Rural District Council, meetings being held in the old Poor Law institution at Droxford.[16] Her very first meeting left a lasting impression.

As I opened the door there was talking and laughing,

---

[16] Ibid, 35

with plenty of smoke from the pipes, but as I appeared all 27 went quiet. One kindly man near the door indicated that my seat was at the top end of the long table and I shall always remember how long the walk seemed before I reached it. The silence persisted until the chairman, a friendly-looking elderly man, welcomed me. I had prepared quite a nice speech, but not a word did I utter as I looked around at those sitting on the hard chairs, their pipes laid down not knowing whether to smoke or not now a lady was present. All I could whisper was: "please all go on smoking", which they thankfully did.

Next to me sat a man who took snuff. It fascinated me as I had never seen anyone do this before. He never seemed to wait for a suitable pause in the proceedings, but helped himself whenever he felt inclined … We had three clergymen, one of whom always arrived in a long voluminous cloak with a black brimmed hat. He looked as though he had stepped out of a history book. The majority were farmers, with a few officers and naval people.[17]

Housing and public health in those days were the main concerns, she was to recall, together with complaints from various villages, the emptying of cesspits and receiving health reports from around the district. Party politics rarely entered into the discussions, with meetings lasting no more than two hours.

---

[17] Op cit, 30

At home, as well as seeing to the children and supervising the running the house, she'd play bridge with cousins Frank and Lillian Birchall. Her favourite game, though, was Bezique, often by herself with a double pack of cards. She was also a keen reader despite having trouble with her eyesight, her favourite author being Somerset Maugham. No one could write about women as well as he could she claimed. She wrote to tell him so. And received a reply.

Then there was her involvement with the Over Sixties Club and Women's Institute, which met regularly at the church hall, talks, quizzes, discussion and demonstrations being the main fare. The family were often roped in to help: Brian to give a recitation and I picked wild flowers from pathways and roadside verges in a competition to see who could collect the greatest variety. The local dramatic society gave a performance of *The Cookery Class* at Corhampton, there were shopping expeditions to Portsmouth and Southsea, scandal when a book was returned to Winchester as "not fit to be read", frequent visits to and from the Warwicks of Gravel Hill, as well as to the cinema. *Clive of India; Old Bones of the River; Lost Horizon; The Sun Never Sets; Pygmalion* were a few of the films she mentions.

There was also the annual holiday at Hayling Island. Each year Father rented a house – Sea View – near the beach where we took ourselves, together with Granny Bennett, and occasionally my sister Mary's companion, Doreen Ware, for a month in August whilst he remained to run the business, visiting us at weekends or whenever he could. We also had a beach hut on the seashore where Granny, still active in her seventies, taught my brothers how to swim.

Aged two at Hayling Island, 1938

Mother was a firm believer maintaining social norms, which ironically at that time meant adhering to the superiority of men. Not something that she spoke about often, never in public, but this came out frequently in discussions we had over the years. Issues arising at the council meetings would be gone over endlessly with my father on her return, not that I understood much of this. One of her favourite anecdotes regarded the appointment of a new music teacher for a primary school. All sorts of questions had been put to one of the candidates, obviously the chairman's favourite. Mother had been unable to get a word in edgeways till finally she scribbled "ask him what instrument he plays" on a piece of paper and handed it across. The chairman took it and placed it to one side. A few minutes later absentmindedly he struck a match, took the note, folded into a spill and used it to light his pipe. The question remained unasked and the candidate appointed. Fine, until his first day at the new school, when chaos broke loose. That morning's welcoming assembly could not take place. Nor any that followed. Not only was the newly-appointed teacher unable to play the piano, he could not manage any other instrument either!

The school at which Mother had been persuaded to teach soon after she arrived in Wickham was affiliated to the church. Whilst she was there it won several prizes for Religious Instruction, or Divinity as it was sometimes called, the Bible playing far greater part in everyday life than it does today. So familiar, in fact, that quotations from both the Old and New Testaments were dropped into everyday conversation alongside catchphrases from the radio: "Drawing a bow at a venture" (taking a chance); "after that the woman died also" (your explanation has gone on long enough); "a cloud no bigger than a man's hand" (the very first intimations of something to happen in the future). "Speak, Lord, for thy servant heareth" a later headmaster would demand of any wrong-doer brought before him; and "Saul has slain his thousands, and David his tens of thousands", after a particularly fine spell of bowling against a rival school.[18] This became problematic as a generation grew up less familiar with the Scriptures. I remember my father being taken literally and accused of insolence when suggesting someone had tackled a problem with "the jawbone of an ass" [*Judges, xv, 16*) (impetuously, head-on).

Mother went a stage further, firmly believing in the literal truth of the Scriptures. No amount of persuasion from any of the more liberal-minded clergy could persuade her otherwise. She did, however, waver over one idea of the Old Testament ideas, incorporated in a number of the hymns we sang each Sunday, eg:

> He gave us eyes to see with
> And lips that we might tell,
> How great is God almighty
> Who has made all things well

"I find it difficult," she told a visiting curate, "to believe in a God who created us merely in order that he might be worshipped."

QUITE A BIT of her time was also taken up helping out

---

with the running of the business: banking, auditing, preparing weekly accounts, socializing with customers and so on. She'd adopted an individual style of shorthand in order to do so. The shop across the Square was next door to Cousin Birchall's pharmacy. Father spent a good deal of his time in the back office, a small room awash with papers of all kinds, huddled over the roll-top desk I was eventually to inherit. Here, as I grew older, I would report each Saturday morning to collect and sign a receipt for my 6d a week pocket-money. "It's a poor family that can't afford one gentleman," he'd sigh as – many years later – he wrote out a cheque to cover my student expenses.

Most fathers find difficulty in reconciling the ways they were raised with those of the current generation. A perennial problem, especially so for anyone brought up in Victorian period, imbued with a strict religious faith at a time when rigidity in such matters was loosening; particularly when followed by the conflicting values of two world wars. Mine was no different: straightforward, a man of great probity, like Mother he had a strong faith exemplified by the poster hung in his dressing-room, where he could see it each morning he shaved. *As for Me and My House, We are for the Lord* it proclaimed. He was, in fact, the perfect candidate for the post of church treasurer, which he held for many years.

Two pieces of advice of advice Father frequently drummed into me were stay clear of gambling and "never talk about yourself." The former came from long business experience; the latter I always found strange. This could have derived from reactions he got through his fearlessness in speaking out about what he saw as injustice – earning him the sobriquet

"Cromwell of Wickham". And, looking back, I get the impression, he was as conscious as my Mother of the class divisions that existed at that time; the stigma of having made his money through enterprise and hard work; of being "in trade".

By now he was an "Agricultural Merchant" rather than an ironmonger. Business would be steady throughout the year with seed potatoes always in demand during the winter, scythes, sickles, cutting implements of all kinds at harvest time and punnets – made of wood shaved down to the thinness of cardboard at the Swanwick Basket Factory – in the strawberry season. The fruit would be sent all over the country via the Meon Valley Line, extra carriages being added with specially constructed shelves. In the early days these were packed down with bracken so that the cargo would arrive undamaged.

Larger orders to the business arrived via road or rail any time of the day and night to be stored in a number of tin-roofed sheds stretching back almost as far as the river. Smaller items were on sale to the general public at the front of the shop. Screws, nails, nuts and bolts were not hermetically sealed in plastic bags in those days; you could buy as few or as many as you wanted. Here it was I learnt my *avoirdupois* table the practical way through weighing loose items out on the scales and depositing them in brown paper bags of appropriate sizes. I also became resident expert as to which of the many wicks on sale were suitable for each particular make of oil lamp, particularly important at a time when few houses were lit by electricity. Garden and farm implements, hoes, rakes, spades, wheelbarrows and the like, were spread out on the pavement in front of the shop, whilst Mr Edwards regularly delivered oil, paraffin, wicks, nails, and a whole range of farm and household utensils from a lorry to all parts of the area. We also had a stall each Monday at Fareham Market.

Father had the contract to supply *Lawes* fertilizers locally, whilst his military experience coupled with business acumen landed an unusual but lucrative commission. The army kept a large number of horses for the transport of guns, ammunition wagons, ceremonial parades and so on. These were stabled in barracks around the area, producing a large amount of manure that needed to be disposed of. Rich in nutrients as well. Just what farmers in a predominantly agricultural area needed – mushroom-growers in particular.

Part of Father's job in the pay corps had been going round various camps checking up on their accounts; ensuring their books balanced. He'd got to know each of the barracks well, together with their personnel and something of their financial problems in disposing of the animals' output. It did not take him long to clinch a deal. This involved them keeping the stables cleared on a weekly basis, three ex-army lorries together with unwilling recruits stationed at the ready, manure supplied to those who needed it within four days, "hot from the horse" as his customers put it. The welfare of the horses greatly improved, a win-win outcome for all concerned. To say nothing of an excellent business deal.

Work and relaxation often intermingled. Quite often we'd be taken out for drives in the car, a Morris 12, registration BCR 640; the scenario always similar. A great display would be made about the trip, how we were going into the country, Father knew just the place, wouldn't it be good to visit such-and-such once more, or maybe this was to be a mystery tour. Off we'd set, my mother in the front and us children at the back, gradually the scenery becoming ever more familiar, mother increasingly suspicious. "This isn't a business trip, is it?" she'd demand. "You haven't brought us all this way just to see Mr ——"? Invariably it was. My father would become intent on navigating the vehicle through the country lanes, distracted apparently bypassing traffic, until to her dismay we pulled into a customer's farmyard, a silage depot, *Lawes Fertilizer Manufacturer's* in Reading or the *Swanwick Basket Factory*. "Won't be a minute" he assured us as, collecting his bone-headed stick from the boot, he disappeared for anything from twenty minutes to an hour. With all her commitments, it's surprising that Mother never learnt to drive. Or so she always maintained. But on 26 May 1939, she records a Mr Grapham giving her lessons and in June she hopes to take her driving test. Nothing came of this, nor did it for eighteen years when, on my father's death, she took to the road and passed the test first time. In the meantime she was to take up cycling instead.

THOUGH HARDLY MENTIONED in the diary, life continued as normal throughout this period while war was increasingly imminent. One of Wickham's last great peacetime occasions, for example, was a pageant, held in the grounds of Rookesbury Park in 1938/9. Almost the whole village, including both my brothers and sister took part, photographed along with the rest of the cast in what appears to be Georgian costumes. The final months of the peace, though, remained in her memory through three very different events.

In June, together with Father, she attendance a national conference on local government at Torquay. Highlights included their stay at the *Palm Court Hotel,* a trip up the river Dart, and a performance of the Pierrot show, *fol-de-rols.* On return Mother set off almost immediately for a trip to Paris, along with Granny Bennett, staying with the Valleries family, with whom Mary was an *au pair.* There was an excursion up the Seine, visits to all the usual sites including Versailles, and a performance at the *Follies Bergères,* which got a good review. Father – strict on such matters – not being with them, they visited the casino, which – in any case – she declared "rotten"!

Then, on 5th August the family – mother, my two brothers, Granny Bennett, Annie Birchall and myself – began an extended holiday at Hayling Island. The weather was perfect and Father came over on his motorbike to join us whenever the business made this possible. Brian and Dick spent most of the day in the water. Granny – now in her eighties – also took a dip although the beaches were almost too crowded to swim. But, on 23rd August the Russian/German pact was signed.

"Very grave news," commented Mother, "war is almost inevitable."

Father thought otherwise, but the church at Hayling that Sunday was full. Paddling was forbidden, the beaches suddenly emptied, Granny was sent post-haste back to Preston and the rest of us returned to Wickham. The date was 31st August.

Behind the scene, as member of the RDC Mother had been closely involved in the planning for any such contingency. Discussions had begun as early as 24th and 28th January; responsibilities allocated for each sector. Colonel Macdonald, having had experience in World War One, was put in charge of Civil Defence, Fire Services, etc, together with Captain Morgan. Mrs MacDonald headed Welfare Services, whilst Mother was appointed billeting officer for the district alongside my godfather, Mr A.E. Roberts. The committee they headed was first held on 1st May and continued to meet regularly from that date onwards.

The two of them worked through till midnight on 31st; canvassing for host families with 1st September set for evacuation day should war be declared. As it was two days later.

The Home Guard marching past the church, c. 1943
(The Stan Woodford Collection, courtesy of Wickham Parish Council)

CHAPTER SIX

WARTIME WICKHAM

MOTHER WAS CALLED to the Council Offices at Bishops Waltham the day war was declared, catching the announcement over the radio. She recalls:

> that strange bewildering moment, and the silence that followed; it was one of the most dramatic moments of my life ... Gone forever were the peaceful meetings at Droxford, for during the next few years everything was filled with a feeling of speed and urgency. The whole council seemed to come to life ... We did not know what to expect, but did our best to be prepared for any eventuality.[19]

If previously family life had been busy it now became frenetic. Among her first tasks on the council was the planning of air raid shelters, including the one built outside Wentworth which remained in place for a good decade after the war. Her prime concern, though, was the evacuation of children, initially from London, among whom were five she took directly into the house. Others were accompanied

---

[19] Warwick, 1982, 21

by their teachers; small babies with their mothers. Suitable accommodation was needed, the collection of blankets and miscellaneous bedding arranged and the reliability of those volunteering to take part in the scheme checked. Some needed persuasion before agreeing to do so. The first contingent, 110 of the expected 180, arrived in the bitter cold on 2nd September, seventy having been mis-recorded en route and remained in the Church Hall prior to the allocation of billets.

The teachers who accompanied the evacuees turned out to be a disappointing lot, mostly unwilling to help. Nor was the rector any more accommodating. The village was full of troops lined up ready for embarkation and there was a stormy meeting after he'd refused them access to the church hall. Eventually they were billeted in the school. By October both the Church and Victory Halls were full to capacity. A further four hundred evacuees arrived on the 11th, fifty-seven of whom were allocated to Wickham, an additional 250 on December 3rd, bombed out of their homes in Southampton, where the Civic Centre had been destroyed. The children were taught in the village school morning and afternoon, on a rota with the regular pupils whilst, as a last resort, the controversial decision was taken to erect a number of small pre-fabricated buildings opposite the Church Hall on School Road. This was intended as a temporary measure to house the overspill, but they remained standing for several years after the war.

Meanwhile, Mother was kept continuously running to the door as relatives from nearby cities sought accommodation for their offspring. The drawing room was hurriedly fitted out with single beds for three such children. But there were more direct homely duties to be seen to. The house needed cleaning, the floors swept with an ancient *Goblin* vacuum cleaner, our clothes hand-washed the old-fashioned way, socks to be darned, shirts and trousers to be patched. Occasionally, the sewing machine would be brought out and Mother would run-up a skirt or blouse from one of several pattern-books. If not, there was the reliable Mrs Duffin a few doors down from the *King's Head* to oblige. Then there were meals to be prepared for whoever was at home; later a daily packed lunch when I began school. All achieved with the assistance of a series of domestic helps of varying reliability: Elsie, Joan, Phyllis, Maisie, Margaret and my favourite, Betty. Part of their responsibility became making my tea and keeping an eye on me till Mother returned from her various meetings in the evening. Jam making and the bottling fruit remained her own preserve; on one occasion producing 72lbs of marmalade from a rare delivery of oranges, Meanwhile Mr Sadler – who I remember with great affection – provided us with fresh fruit and vegetables from the large garden.

My father was just as busy. As well as his normal work at the shop, he'd been asked to help with the National Registration, a census conducted house-to-house prior to the production of ration and identity cards. This took up quite a bit of his time. Occasionally he was out on the rounds in the mobile van, there was our stall at Fareham Market each Monday, regular attendance at the Masonic Lodge. And now he joined the Local Defence Volunteers – soon to be renamed the Home Guard. One of the earliest tasks for the Wickham contingent entailed the gathering of scrap iron or palings for use in the manufacture of planes or armament, the iron railings in front of Wentworth coming under immediate threat, as they continued to be for some time.

Throughout May and June 1940, whilst our troops retreated and France capitulated, there were frequent reports of raids on the south coast; planes brought down in the Solent. Invasion seemed almost certain. The pupils of Rookesbury Park School had by now moved to the west country, the incoming military contingent supplying mains water and electricity. Meanwhile, the navy had taken over one of Wickham's largest properties, Beverley, as a maternity unit. The family made the trip to Hayling to bring home our possessions from the beach hut, due for demolition to make place for guns. Gas masks and identity wrist-straps had been issued, an air-raid shelter dug outside the Studio and Mother began stocking up on rice, tinned vegetables, dried fruit, etc some of which remained in store well into the 1960s.

The situation had become critical enough for Father to gather us together for a family conference. He and Mother would be making their wills. There was a suggestion that the rest of us might move to a safer area, with Bloxham less dangerously situated for my brother's secondary education than Lancing. Before leaving they were presented with sheath knifes, their initials engraved on the hilt. A "coming of age" symbol, I assumed. For carving wood; sharpening pencils; digging out weeds perhaps? Their real purpose only emerged within the last few years; from notes Dick left behind on the computer following his death. The gift had been accompanied by Father's chilling advice. Should Invasion take place, my brothers confronted by the enemy, they should follow Churchill's suggestion; to "take one of them with you." The same notes recall groups of 16 to 18-year-olds armed in this way "never contacting one another … so that if captured the information divulged was limited." My brother's knife remains in the family.

Behind the scenes, whilst mother attended meetings to oversee all aspects of the community's response, the village prepared itself for expected enemy assault. The bridge between Knowle and Wickham was decommissioned, signposts were removed in case they aided the enemy advance, a dummy enplanement set up to draw bombers away from the main cities. Holes were drilled in major roads into which metal rods could be slotted to impede the enemy's advance; concrete blocks known as "Dragon's teeth" appeared in strategic places for the same purpose. Shelters were erected and practice in responding to sirens began. Wickham's took 2½ minutes. A wavy, undulating wail meant enemy bombers sighted; the all clear signalled by a single continuous pitch. ARP (Air raid precautions) became a regular way of life: blackout, with tin-hatted wardens appointed to make sure this was in place; SWS (static water supplies) made regularly available; sand buckets together with long handled shovels readily (in order to keep one's distance whilst dousing incendiary bombs) on hand.

War had been declared at 11am on Sunday 3 September and from then on became an ever-present factor throughout the diaries – sometimes close, sometimes far off – overshadowing all other events. Not all of our successes and failures are commented on directly, but the ebb and flow of events can be traced in outline.

FIRST TO BE mentioned is an English ship torpedoed in the channel on 4th September. Further vessels were sunk that month, including the *Courageous*, with 1200 men aboard, only 640 of whom were saved. From then on, matters were recoded as going from bad to worse:

12th November, the Armistice Service cancelled;

18th December, the *Graff Spey* scuppered;

April, 1940, British expeditionary force sent to support Norway forced into ignominious retreat;

8th May, Chamberlain resigns, Churchill becomes Prime Minister;

13th May, the Germans sweep into Belgium and Holland; both countries capitulate with their Royal families seeking refuge over here;

16th May, enormous German advances in France;

26th May, day of national prayer;

27th May, ill feeling regarding the Belgian King's surrender;

30th May, British Expeditionary Force surrounded, 40% rescued at Dunkirk;

14th June, the Germans parade through Paris, followed by a second day of prayer throughout Britain.

17th June, France asks Germany for peace terms; "we are left", Mother writes, "to fight it out on our own."

But it was not until just after midnight on 24th June that the Wickham siren sounded and we spent our first night down in the cellar, getting what sleep we could on camp beds or deckchairs. Coal was now being delivered to the old engine room but the remnants, dust and aroma remained, none of which made the atmosphere any more pleasant. Two hours only on that occasion, but it became a regular occurrence, night and day, often three or four times in succession. July was particularly stressful with only eight raid-free days throughout the month. Wickham was obviously not a main target. It was, though, perilously close to Portsmouth, which had a single bridge connecting it to the mainland, and Southampton, with its docks and factories – especially that of the Supermarine spitfire – both obvious targets for attack. As were the airfields at Gosport and Lee-on-Solent, just a few miles away, whilst Southwick, at the foot of Portsdown Hill, was to become headquarters of Allied Command. And always the chance that someone's blackout was not all that it might have been. After this came the Blitz, the wholesale bombing of London and the rest of our cities. Mother notes especially the damage inflicted on Buckingham Palace on 12th September, the chapel destroyed on 16th and six Wren churches on 27th December. This phase of the war culminated in the Battle of Britain in May 1940.

Down in our cellar bunkbeds were installed, providing minimum comfort; later a Morrison shelter. Memories of the raids are sketchy but vivid. I recall the wailing of the sirens, being hurried downstairs, the drone of incoming aircraft, my brothers arguing first as to whether they were 'ours' or 'theirs', fighters or bombers (although even I could tell these apart), – that having been established – their precise make, type and destination. But nothing ever quite evaded the damp chill, nor memory of the hours spent in this dismal worm-infested cavern, staring up night-after-night at the ceiling illuminated by the light of a dim bulb swinging from a single flex. Vague

71

shadows danced about the walls. Cracks and crevices formed images imprinted to this day in my mind: a flower-seller, basket by her side, a large pole stretched across her lap; the roundel of a heavily-cratered full-moon; a bull with jutting horns – the twin of those I was later to learn can be found in the caves of Lascaux and Altimero.

Emerging into daylight after such raids we'd sometimes find the countryside strewn with thin metallic streamers, black on one, side silver on the other. These had been dropped by the RAF to interrupt communication between incoming planes or the enemy to scramble our radar system. Leaving the house during an air raid was inadvisable, shrapnel from damaged aircraft being a constant hazard. Even when the all-clear had sounded one was not completely safe. We were constantly warned not to pick up any toys or fruit lying by the wayside; could be they were packed with explosives dropped from enemy bombers. On at least two occasions there was an unexpected raid whilst out walking and we had to find somewhere to take shelter. And once the siren sounded whilst we were looking after the stall in Fareham Market. Father up-ended a large circular corrugated zinc trough, used for feeding a large number of pigs, and heaved me into it. Above us a tight formation of German bombers droned inexorably across the sky, with seemingly less disciplined British fighters weaving in and out between them. On another occasion I was playing in the garden when, completely without warning, an enormous aircraft roared above me at rooftop height. The noise was deafening and, as I flung myself down on the lawn, before it swept away over the village, I saw black cross markings on its wings. One of theirs!

Compared with the devastation that befell Portsmouth, Southampton and other great cities, the village suffered little loss of life or damage to property during the war. Mother recorded some, but not all of it. On July 15 1940, one of our planes was brought down at Swales farm; on 12th August an enemy bomber crashed with three of the crew parachuting to safety, and on 28th Knowle was bombed as was Rooksbury. The following night one of our planes came down at Mr Roberts farm. The most dramatic incident I personally re-member was a lorry full of ammunition catching fire at the top of Hoad's Hill and exploding to send shells and debris shooting in all directions.

Rookesbury House

THROUGHOUT THE YEAR there was talk of me and my brothers being moved to a safer area. Rationing was also becoming a major concern. This was to vary throughout the war, but at the outset consisted of one egg and two ounces of tea and butter per person per week, an ounce of cheese, eight ounces of sugar, four ounces of bacon and four ounces of margarine. Wentworth was fortunate in having a large garden in which we could grow our own fruit and vegetables, additional supplies being available from Frith Farm and the Gravel Hill nurseries. Frozen food had not yet arrived on the scene, but eggs were preserved in a transparent glutinous substance (sodium silicate) called water glass. Items such as whale meat, spam, dried apricot rings, tapioca, and acorn coffee became part of our normal diet. For me, the only young child in the family, this was later to be supplemented by a daily dose of concentrated orange juice, to which water was added, and a ghastly spoonful of cod-liver oil – both introduced by the Ministry of Food under the Welfare Food Scheme.

The weather itself seemed to reflect the general mood of despondency. 1940 brought snow lying two feet deep with coal rationed to 2½ tons per annum. People were marooned in the floods, but there was skating on Rookesbury Pond. On 30th January came one of the worst storms Mother could remember. She hurried up to Preston, no mean feat at this this time with two changes of train – at Alton on the Meon Valley line[20], then LMS (London, Midlands, Scotland) – where at Cop Lane the pipes had burst. Back home the roads

---

[20] See: Stone, 1983

were impassable, telegraph poles were down; at Wentworth, water was coming from the roof in four places.

This was the year when Wickham's Home Guard, under the leadership of General Sir Herbert Powell, swung fully into action. The General had spent many years as commander of the Gurkha Rifles in India before retiring to Lower House, on the Winchester Road. A section of the regiment taking part in King George VI's coronation had come down to parade through the Square in his honour. Now there were to be regular patrols on the watch for enemy paratroopers or unexploded bombs, rifle practice on the range at Knowle, drill to keep the men fit, kit inspections to ensure they were adequately equipped and public demonstrations of their prowess. Dress rehearsals for expected invasion were staged: manoeuvres on Wickham Common, for example, the defence not only of the general's own home but Titchfield barrage balloon station, the "capture" of the local reservoir, and the famous occasion on 25 May 1941, when Southwick Home Guard mounted an attack on Wickham itself.

Besides the Home Guard, Wickham's contribution to the war effort consisted of a group of women who met regularly at Lady Bird's house on Winchester Road (later a convent) sorting nuts and bolts from crashed aircraft to be reused in the manufacture of new planes. The somewhat chauvinist notice pinned to one of the walls pronounced: "A little talk stops a lot of work." A similar group under the aegis of the WVS (Women's Voluntary Service) met in the Southdown Garage adjacent to the railway station, attaching strips of multicoloured material to nets hung from the ceiling in the production of camouflage. The village also helped out in less direct ways. Throughout the war a series of *Weapons Weeks* were held to raise money for the armed forces.

Activities such as these were known as the "Home Front", the village being kept well supplied with government posters encouraging our participation – *Dig for Victory, Make do and Mend, Lend a Hand on the Land,* for example. My favourites as a child were the exploits of an orange-coloured anthropomorphic vegetable *Dr Carrott*, aimed at cultivating a balanced diet and *Beware the Squander Bug.* This ghastly, green, multi-legged little creature covered in swastikas was supposed to encourage thrift. I don't know how successful it was in this respect, but he succeeded in putting the frighteners on me.

By now, though, one of Mother's main contributions to the war effort – as billeting officer – had begun in earnest.

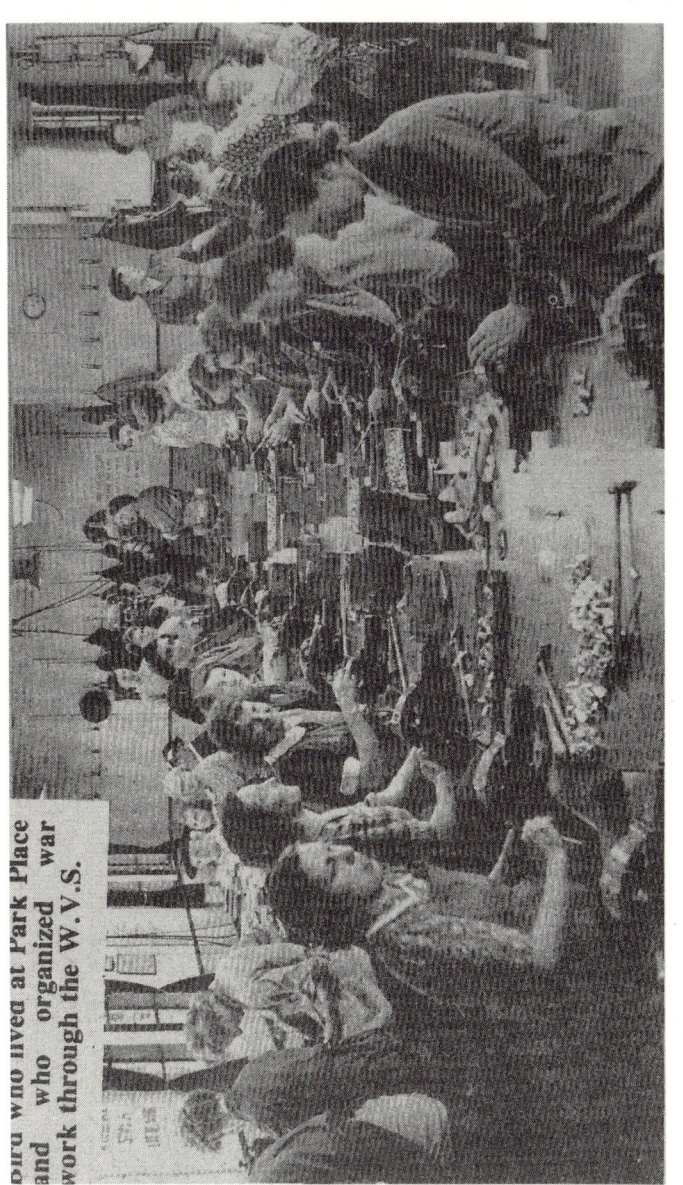

Sorting spare metal as part of the war effort, c. 1941 (courtesy of The News, Portsmouth)

...bird who lived at Park Place and who organized war work through the W.V.S.

CHAPTER SEVEN

HOMES FROM HOME – THE EVACUEES

HOWEVER WILLING THE hosts or the care taken in planning, the influx of large numbers of strangers into any community is bound to lead to problems. The arrival of the evacuees on 2 September 1939 was no exception, and Mother was fortunate in having Mr A.E. Roberts – a close friend and colleague on the District Council – as a partner.

He was also my godfather and one of the most charismatic people I've ever met. He'd started in the fruit-farming business at the age of 17, was called up for military service at the outset of the First World War, captured by the Germans but made a daring escape from the prisoner of war camp. Palling up with a fellow prisoner and a local fräulein, they dressed as locals for the first part of the escapade, with replicas of their guard's uniforms in their backpacks for the second. They did not get far before they were apprehended and their belongings searched. All might still have gone well had not one of the uniforms been intended for his 6' 2" companion. Checking the records, his captors discovered none of the camp guards was that tall and sent them back. At the end of the war he and other POWs were feted at a banquet in Hull, but when the mayor gave a patronizing speech praising their efforts the man was shouted down. A sign of the way attitudes were changing; "A cloud no bigger than a man's hand"? Well, maybe.

In 1926 he took over Frith Farm, building it up to the point where he supplied fruit to Woolworths on a national basis, and pioneered the cultivation of loganberries in this country. He also remembered an inscription he'd seen whilst hiding in a churchyard during his wartime adventures. *Count that Day Lost whose Low Descending Sun views from thy hand no worthy action done*, it read, and Mr Roberts took this to heart. He ran the local scout groups, whilst red faced, jovial, speaking with the most distinctive of sing-song voices, a dedicated *Man of the Trees,* he was frequently to be seen striding around the village offering words of comfort or encouragement, always able to step in with the most practical advice. And, printed in green at the foot of his distinctive yellow notepaper, embellished with the signature – also in green – was that self-same maxim.

Appropriately, the testimonial presented to him by the council on retirement referred to his "rugged individuality, his intolerance of petty bureaucracy, his tireless efforts to beautify the district and his undoubted energy and unfailing courtesy". This was accompanied by an illuminated scroll showing Mr Roberts with dustpan-and-brush, reminding him of the many times he'd swept the bus shelter when no one else would do it; trees, which he'd insisted should adorn all council estates; the scouting emblem, whose uniform he wore with pride well into his 60s.

An evacuee inspection, Mr Roberts 2nd on left with clipboard, c. 1942 (Betty Rudd Collection, courtesy of Wickham History Society)

Mr Roberts' brisk, outgoing no-nonsense attitude, coupled with Mother's reserved, more measured approach; her insights gained from bringing up a large family, meant they worked well as a team.

For her part, the role of billeting officer impinged upon home life. At the beginning of 1941 Wentworth, like most other large houses, was full to capacity. In term time two boys aged 11 and 13 slept in the back room at the top of the house whilst two families occupied the front two bedrooms facing the square. Father, Mother and I were in the large bedroom on the second floor at the front; between four and six children in my brothers' bedroom to the rear. They would be relocated in the holidays when Brian and Dick returned home, or slept on camp beds in the drawing room. And all this while a further family crammed into the one remaining bedroom in part of the whole wing that would be separated from the rest of the house in the post-war years.

Inevitably, difficulties arose. Mary, arriving unexpectedly, was not best pleased to find strangers sleeping in her top floor room. Father often returned late at night from Home Guard duties and had to make-do downstairs so as not to wake the household. Occasionally Wentworth was so crowded that use had to be made of the outside air raid shelter in the square just opposite.

Meanwhile, the arrival of a large number in such a small village led to wider issues, not least making sure families not billeted, or those in transit, were fed. National policy had been the establishment of centres for such purpose, introduced soon after the beginning of the war, further developed in March 1941, with Wickham being selected as one of the experimental areas. A tremendous row ensued with the closing the Victory Hall at certain times of the day so that it could be used as a communal dining-room. And for some of the evacuees, it all proved too much.

Once, after a heavy raid on London, a train full of the evacuees arrived at the station. It was very difficult to find homes for them all as by this time almost every available place field. In fact we did not accomplish this task until the early hours of the morning, when we returned home successful but exhausted. Alas, on visiting the homes next morning to see that all were happily settled in, we found to our dismay that the majority had returned to London on the first train, saying they would rather face the bombs in London than live in such a quiet place as Wickham where there was nothing to do![21]

Another problem was finding billets for expectant mothers or those with small children. The solution was to requisition Bridge House behind Chesapeake Mill and the appointment of a qualified Warden to look after them. Beneficial though it was, this led to continuous problems in the years to come. A dozen or so women sharing a single kitchen inevitably led to minor disturbances; disputes and petty jealousies often led to blows. Bridge house also became of great interest to sailors on shore leave. Quite often, having gone through their payroll, they'd refuse to leave and the two billeting officers would be called out at all hours of the night to deal with the situation, Mother gently trying to persuade the men to depart; Mr Roberts dealing with them in a direct man-to-man manner. He would then call the women together for an avuncular talk about mending their ways, concluding with their kneeling down before him and promising never to repeat their misdeeds. A vow they always kept – till the next time.

On a happier note, in December 1940 a "toy service" was held in the parish church especially for evacuated children and the system of exchange of clothing – which was to

---

[21] Warwick, 1982, 27

continue throughout the war – established in the Victory Hall. Garments of all shapes and sizes were included, right down to the smallest, which were donated for dolls' dresses.

It was also agreed that a women's club for evacuees should be opened. Mother became the treasurer and meetings were held regularly at the church hall. This would also be used on temporary basis in cases of emergency, as when in April at the height of the bombing a train load of families arrived from London and were bedded out there until adequate billeting could be found. Three days later one of the children contracted measles. An ambulance arrived but the mother refused to allow him, or any of his four brothers, to be moved. The local magistrate was sent for, as was the RSPCC, but she remained adamant and the law – apparently – was on her side. Every other family had to be moved and they had the premises to themselves for three whole weeks at a time when accommodation was badly needed. And then the whole building had to be thoroughly fumigated before returning to its normal use.

Much closer to home was the tragedy of the Blake family, who transferred from the Rectory to Wentworth in the early weeks of the war. The father was a senior officer in the navy and they had one son, Michael. Mr Blake was called north to Scappa Flow, the Scottish base, following a successful enemy raid that October. Whilst he was away, Michael, who'd been playing in the Square with Teddy, another evacuee, chased him across the road where he was knocked down and killed by a car. Soon afterwards, the Blakes left the village.

The accident is recorded in her diary, but two more personal cases with which my mother had to deal were to remain long in her memory. The first was a four-year-old girl who arrived among many others on the train from London with neither documentation nor luggage. All she could say was that her name was Sheila. Mother took her into the house and she lived with us as one of the family till the end of the war. Then, just as we were about to adopt her, an aunt appeared from nowhere to claim her. It was heartbreaking for all concerned when she had to leave. Then there were the three little boys aged four, six and seven whose father – like so many others – came knocking on the door asking if we could take them in. He was in submarines; his wife had left him and Mother agreed. Some months later he returned on leave, saw how happy the children were, and begged her to keep them together if anything happened to him. It was a request impossible to refuse and, when six months later the submarine was lost, they remained with us, again as part of the family. Once more, it was not until many months later that the grandmother appeared and agreed to look after them. Individual requests such as this mounted and eventually a notice had to be fixed to the front of house providing hours when consultation would be available.

Bridge House seemed to feature largely in my mother's diaries throughout the war. A far more harrowing scene, which was to live with Mother forever, occurred there on 14 May 1941, when one of the women there left her two small sons alone whilst she did the laundry. The elder, aged four, climbed onto a chair and reached down a bottle of disinfectant (carbolic acid) which he gave his two-year-old brother, Roy, to drink. The child was rushed to Wentworth house, the doctor was called, but nothing could be done and he died an hour later. The postmortem recorded a verdict of Accidental Death. Two months later his brother, Alan, was awarded second prize in a Baby Show, but in October the father was expelled from the House after a milk-throwing incident. And there I'd thought the story of Bridge House had ended. Until, on a recent visit, I heard tell of disembodied children's voices, spectral apparitions appearing to those staying there ...

Wickham Home Guard defending the general's house, c. 1941
(courtesy of The News, Portsmouth)

CHAPTER EIGHT

HOME & AWAY

BY NOW THE war was going badly on a number of fronts. On 3 June 1940, 40% of the British Expeditionary Force had been rescued from Dunkirk. Hitler had turned his attention to Russia and the Germans were advancing on our new allies in Moscow. We were fighting a rearguard action against Rommel in Africa, a parachute raid on Crete had ended in disaster, and the Japanese entered the war sweeping all before them, capturing Singapore on 16th February. Each reported spasmodically in the diaries, vague and incomplete alongside a tally of ships lost throughout the period:

18th July – *Van Dyke*;

31st August – the destroyers *Eske* and *Valentine* sunk by dive bombers in the North Sea;

27th October – the luxury liner *Empress of Britain*, the victim of u-boat 32;

24 May 1941 – the *Hood* sunk;

9th November – a convoy of eight ships sunk in the Mediterranean;

15th November – the *Ark Royal* torpedoed by U Boat 32

The submarine was itself sunk off the Irish coast on 30th October. Nevertheless, the first week that month marked the heaviest loss of shipping since the war began.

Mary was to witness first-hand the result of such carnage when she began her training as a nurse at Wingfield Manor Orthopaedic Hospital, Oxford, prior to a transfer to Middlesex in April 1941. Among her patients were wounded soldiers returning from active service and victims of the Blitz as well as treating burnt airmen at Stoke Mandeville. She was disappointed when she was not permitted to join more experienced staff when they left for the front.

Both my brothers were away during termtime, the village offering very little by way of entertainment for them on their return. By now they were developing into quite different characters and responded accordingly. Brian was by far the more extrovert, full of energy, devoted to the outdoor life and forever getting into scrapes. As I grew up games invariably led to some form of masculine rough and tumble, often ending in tears – for which he'd be immediately crestfallen. He was keen on all sports, horseracing, football and cricket, boxing especially. There was a punchball attached on strong elastic bands, wall-to-ceiling, in one of the back rooms which he'd attack with vigour wearing a special pair of gloves. Practicing, perhaps, for "going one round" with the pugilist in one of the side-shows at the annual fair; a challenge, it's said, he had to be restrained from accepting.

The gift of an airgun on his 15th birthday may appear somewhat irresponsible from a contemporary point of view. This was rural England, though. Times were different and he was a countryman through and through. Besides which, rats were putting paid to the poultry we kept at the top of the garden. Grey squirrels were beginning to oust the red (at one point the government paid a one shilling per head bounty – or rather, per tail, as this was required as evidence), and rabbits were similarly regarded as vermin. The gun, a silver *Diana* with wooden stock, remained in the hall stand till well after the war. For all this, Brian had a sensitive nature. He was deeply moved by his confirmation at Chichester Cathedral on 7 May 1940. There were upsets on leaving home at the beginning of each term but once there did well, especially in Maths, and on 22nd July the following year he was voted "the most popular boy in the school".

He built up a fantastic collection of metal soldiers representing armies of the world in their military regalia, given to him as birthday or Christmas presents over the years. Scrupulous care was kept of them in their original boxes, about a dozen to each. A cheaper range, nondescript, in fighting kit, were set aside for mock battles, many with heads, arms, legs, missing as a result. On VE Day the pukka regiments were set out in marching order in a side window of the shop. At some point thereafter they disappeared, much to his annoyance. Brian's first love, though, was the Navy. He'd spend hours assiduously gluing together and painting prepacked models of battleships of all nations. We also had a copy of *Jane's Fighting Ships,* many of which were lost during the war, which he annotated with precise details – where sunk, when, the fate of the crew, etc. Of all the books at Wentworth, this is the one I most regret missing when the house was cleared after my brother Dick's death in 2018.

One of my favourite childhood memories is Brian's steam

engine. It can't have been more than 6 x 4 inches, with a brass cylinder. This was filled with water before lighting a small burner which ran on methylated spirits. The water would boil, the pistons shoot in and out, turning the wheel. The whole contraption had to be screwed down onto a solid piece of wood or, when fully under steam, it might well have taken off. There was also the danger of the thing exploding, which it occasionally did – especially if the safety-valve was blocked. There'd be a jet of steam, an ear-piercing whistle as everything in the vicinity would be spraying with boiling water. Mother banned it to the back kitchen as it stank the place out. An unforgettable experience.

DICK WAS FAR more reserved by nature, extremely practical; good with his hands which he seemed able to turn to anything. His approach to a problem was thoughtful. Whereas Brian would rush in and apply the first and most obvious solution, Dick would patiently weigh up all the options before tackling it carefully in a methodical manner. A perfect example of this was the *Diana* air rifle. When the manufacturers modified the size of pellets, it was Dick who worked out a solution enabling them to continue using the gun. He'd take hours constructing model planes from tissue paper glued onto a balsa wood framework, their propellors powered by elastic bands or tiny spirit-driven motors. They'd be launched by hand in Blackman's field behind Wentworth, or from long runways of newspaper pinned down to flatten the tall grass. He was at this time a chorister at Chichester Cathedral, where he was confirmed on 17 March 1943, which meant he sometimes missed out on Christmas Day with the family. When this happened we'd celebrate the occasion a few days earlier.

IN SUMMER THERE would always be games in the garden, races, French cricket, hide and seek, bowls and croquet (we had complete sets of each) and, on one occasion, the construction of an elaborate maze from sticks and branches. Rabbits were kept in hutches at the top of garden, a tortoise meandered about the lawn whilst, at one point, chicken had free range of the undergrowth. Occasionally, one of them would go broody, preparing a secret nest and laying copious number of eggs which she attempted to hatch rather than sharing with us. A kind of hide-and-seek ensued, searching out such clandestine stashes; great fun for a five-year-old. Once discovered the genuine eggs would be replaced with white enamel ones. The hens never seemed to notice the difference, returning to their clandestine nests day after day; continuing to lay as we went on making the substitutions. Up to the point where there were so many bogus eggs that everyone had stopped counting. Another problem was hens making a meal of their eggs. Shells filled with mustard and placed in their nest usually put a stop to this.

All very good-natured, if not always for the hens – although on one occasion there was an almighty bust-up. We all thought it was impossible to grow peaches in this country, but Mary planted three such trees at the top of the garden, alongside the wall that separated Wentworth from the Studio. She lovingly tended them over the months until, against all the odds, a single fruit emerged on one of the branches. My sister waited patiently for it to ripen, but was beaten to it by

Brian and Dick who genuinely seemed to think they were doing her favour by picking it and presenting it to her one morning at the breakfast table. Nor could they imagine why she was incandescent with rage as a result!

Indoors, a number of board games were kept in store for rainy days or winter evenings: *Monopoly*, *Totopoly* (lifelike metal horses racing round a board), *Buccaneer* (tiny plastic ships that sailed across the oceans collecting treasure and fighting one another), *Campaign* (battles between miniature armies), to mention but a few. We also had an enormous *Meccano* set with multiple components. Usually, the whole family were involved in such activities – Brian dashing in, quick, daring and seemingly giving little thought to each move, Dick pondering for what seemed hours before deciding what to do, myself insisting on playing whilst knowing nothing of the rules, Mother infuriating everyone by invariably allowing me to win. All of which could lead to violent squabbles. Great care, though, was taken with the components of each game. Carefully removed from their boxes at the beginning and returned to them at the end of each session, they lasted throughout my childhood to be enjoyed by the next generation.

Unfortunately, the puppet theatre did not. This was silver-coloured, measured about 3 by 1½ feet, and was made up of several light wooden sections that slotted together to form the framework. The front consisted of a stage with curtains that pulled aside on strings, the back was open enabling two people to crouch behind manipulating the puppets. These were kept in a cardboard box: *Mr Punch, Judy, Crocodile, Policeman*, etc, with gaudily coloured plaster heads and appropriate clothing; several of them homemade. With Brian and Dick behind the scenes, a puppet on each hand, it was possible to get four characters on stage at the same time. I forget who did each of the voices, ("that's the way to do it!"; "I'm taking you to prison, Mr Punch", etc, etc); and there was a hangman's noose into which Mr P unwittingly thrust his head, a large stick with which he beat Judy, and a string of sausages to be stolen by the dog.

The radio was also a major source of entertainment. All ages and tastes were catered for. On a Saturday night the family gathered round the fireplace in the front room on to listen to a fabulous West Country serial At the Luscombe's, followed by In Town Tonight – interviews with celebrities visiting the capital, and a number of variety programmes. For the younger generation there was Children's Hour, involving *Music and Movement, Toytown, Norman and Henry Bones, Boy-Detectives; Said the Cat to the Dog, The Box of Delights;* for the adults *Saturday Night Theatre, the Radio Doctor,* or *The Brains Trust* featuring the celebrated Professor Joad. From 1946 there would be *Dick Barton, Special Agent,* whilst World Theatre would introduce me to some of the great classics from other nations. Similarly, one could read the content of a lot of the major productions in The Listener.

The gramophone was occasionally brought out. Hardly surprising; it was enormous, heavy, and difficult to carry. The lid would be raised, the handle inserted, its mechanism cranked up. A record was placed on the turntable and the arm lowered gently onto it. With the lid closed we were able to listen to one of a number of 78rpm records, full volume with a couple of doors at the front opened, less so with one of them closed, faint with both shut. And if this was not sufficient one could always cram a sock in for good measure. Among our favourites were *My Brother Makes the Noises for the Talkies, I'm Happy When I'm Hiking, The Laughing Policeman,* mostly dating back to the 1920s, and the inimitable Les Compagnons de la chanson version of *The Three Bells* (the "Jimmy Brown Song"). I don't think we ever bought a new record and these in particular must eventually have been worn to a frazzle.

Reading was important to each of us in different ways. I don't remember any daily newspapers but at weekends there was the *Sunday Dispatch.* Comics were banned, though I looked forward to the weekly edition of Enid Blyton's *Sunny Stories* before persuading my parents to order *KnockOut.* For Brian it was always stories of the sea, Kipling's *Captains Courageous* being one of his favourites; later he graduated to Dornford Yates. Father had a collection of A.G. Street's agricultural publications on the shelf behind his armchair, whilst Mother was fairly eclectic. She ordered the series *Worlds Works* – edited versions of all-time best authors – to be delivered to her regularly, but was especially keen on Somerset Maugham. Hers was a quiet but wicked sense of humour. At about this time she began to be troubled by sore eyes and occasionally asked Father to read to her. The passages she claimed to have reached were invariably those of a sexual nature. My father was quite straitlaced in this respect. "You don't really want to hear this bit, do you?" he'd enquire. Either that or he'd attempt to edit them out completely. Mother, of course, was having none of it, enjoying it all the more as a poor man became increasingly embarrassed.

94

Transport was by now severely restricted. Petrol, previously rationed, became unavailable for all but essential users in July 1942. Trains and buses still took us in and out of Wickham. The former ran on the Meon Valley line, to Alton via Droxford, West Meon, Privett, Tisted, Farringdon, where one could catch an LMS train to London.[22] Buses ran to severely reduced timetables: *Southdown* via Southwick to and from Portsmouth (a spectacular ride over Portsdown Hill on top of a double-decker); *Hants and Dorset* on the Winchester/Fareham circuit. Both services often pulled into the Square with gas cylinders towed behind them to save petrol.

Whole streets in Southsea had been bombed to ruins, Palmerton and King's Road especially, during a raid on 29 May 1941. Nevertheless, we were able to shop for my brothers' school uniform, have our hair cut as usual and take tea at Handley's. A crisis arose when Mother spotted a badly damaged hotel for sale on the seafront going for a song. She wanted to snap it up, but Father – always more cautious – had his doubts. What if the bombers returned to complete their mission; planning permission for the renovation was not granted; prices took a tumble? Eventually he had his way. The hotel not only survived, it flourished; a fact she'd remind him of each time we drove past it in the post-war years. Eventually he'd take elaborate detours to avoid such altercations.

MOTHER ALWAYS HAD a penchant for the theatre. Growing up in Preston her father had taken her to

---

22 See, Stone, 1983

many shows. Now she became just as fond of the cinema. Portsmouth offered many opportunities, some of the cinemas as ornate as any theatre with curtains that pulled aside at the beginning of the main film; others had electronic organs that rose as if by magic at the front of the auditorium playing recent hits or all-time favourites. The words of each song were projected on the screen and we sang along in harmony. Less grand were the *Savoy* and *Embassy* in Fareham[23] both of which remained open throughout the war. Crime was very much to Mother's taste – *Inspector Homleigh, Poison Pen, Blackmail, The Spy in Black*, for example. When accompanied by the children it was all derring-do: *Four Feathers, The Sun Never Sets, Charlie Chan at Treasure Island, Five Came Back*.

Matching up the bus timetables with those of the cinema – printed weekly in the *Hampshire Telegraph and Post* – was always a problem. As was having to take account of possible breakdowns or air raids en route. There was even the occasion when the sirens went after five minutes, the cinema was cleared and we had to sit out the raid amid the stalls in Fareham market. On another the Tarzan film Brian had taken me to see had not arrived so they showed one I'd already seen instead. At the conclusion it was announced the advertised film was now available and we got two for the price of one. There was not much of a problem about this as cinemas then ran a continuous programme. The main feature would be followed by a shorter 'B' movie, trailers for next week's presentations, advertising and newsreels with short intervals

---

[23] Barker et al, pp 43—4

for the selling of drinks, popcorn and ice cream. There was no booking of seats and admittance was permitted at any time. If early one could go in and risk seeing the end of the previous film; if late, clamber over those already there and miss the beginning of what you'd come to see. As the programme were continuous, one could remain in the cinema as long as you wanted, hence the catchphrase "this is where I came in". Most cinemas had two types of seating, the cheaper to the front, often a few rows back from the screen, the more expensive on a balcony or on a gradual incline to the rear. And always there'd be an usherette armed with a torch to show you to a vacant seat.

Locally, there were occasional film shows at the Victory Hall, usually government propaganda shorts (*Dig for Victory; Make do and Mend; Beware the Squanderbug,* etc) togetherer with mini epics highlighting our latest successes – what there were of them. Churchill featured largely, cheered to the rafters or greeted with a stamping of feet. Similarly, a van would pull up in the Square, the back opened up and a range of such material shown free of charge. I was taken to the "real" pictures for first time on 18 April 1940, *The Thief of Baghdad* if I remember correctly, or it might have been *Bambi.* Whichever, Mother reports that I enjoyed it very much, although I protested loudly whenever she covered my eyes during the nasty bits. The family treat in January that year was a visit to the pantomime, *Babes in the Wood* at the Kings Theatre, Southsea, together with the Gravel Hill contingent, all of us crammed into one of the boxes booked specially for the occasion. This was a great success, unlike a later visit which featured the comedians Old Mother Riley and her Daughter Kitty. That show was full of dirty jokes and innuendo. Father was only restrained from leaving the theatre by our protests and my mother's pleas.

Although they could hardly compete, Wickham had its own amateur dramatic group. In 1941 they gave us Aladdin, following this next year with Sleeping Beauty. Fair Day, as already mentioned,[24] was one of the casualties of war. It was about this time that my birthday began to be marked by a special treat. My Godfather, A.E. Roberts, the owner Frith Farm at the top of Mill Lane one year invited me up there to celebrate the occasion in a genuine gypsy caravan he'd bought, and so the tradition began. Right through till his death he'd send me a book, usually something to do with the countryside and always warmly inscribed with a flourish of green ink.

BY THE SUMMER of 1942 both my brothers had graduated from the red three-wheel bicycle they used to share. Dick's was a new one costing £8.18.8. In April they were teaching Mother how to ride on the lawn behind Wentworth and soon all of them they were taking trips together out into the country, including an eight-mile marathon on 21st July with Mary. Two of my brothers' special friends were Kendall Ockenden – with whom Brian was to have any number of scrapes as a teenager – and Bruce Tappenden, who later wrote a history of the village.[25] Now that the family were more mobile, visits to Gravel Hill – part of which had been taken over

---

[24] See also Chapter Four
[25] Tappenden, 1996

for the manufacture of spare parts for aircraft – became more frequent. Uncle Will, who must have been about Father's age was said to have helped lay the foundation stone of the house at the age of four. He was loud-voiced and hearty with enormous eyebrows and a penchant for nicknames, flirting with the ladies and generally taking a rise out of all and sundry. Unsurprisingly, and partly down to his initials – William Arthur Gale – he was widely known as "Wag."

Auntie Emma, who had a deformed thumb as a result of an accident with the mangle some years back, was completely deaf. She wore the most extraordinary hearing-aid consisting of two tortoiseshell trumpets, set like rams' horns on either side of her head, curving round to be inserted into each ear. She sang continuously without words, a tuneless "la-la-la" – the only person I've known do so outside the pages of a book.

Father's business had made steady progress over the years. From the ironmonger's shop at the corner of the square and the stall in Fareham market to the development into an agricultural merchant, the building of Preston Ridge and the acquisition of Wentworth house, both testaments to his success. As was the next step. Following naturally from his line of business came the purchase of Botley Manor Farm, sold by auction for £64,000 at *The Dolphin Hotel* on 26 September 1941, opening up a new and exciting venture for all of us.

St Nicholas Parish Church and the elementary school
(now demolished)

CHAPTER NINE

THE JANUS YEARS

THE FARM WAS all that one could imagine. Straight from the picture books in fact: a central all-purpose yard surrounded by a couple of barns – one thatched, the other tiled – an outhouse and a series of fenced-off pigsties. To one side stood the white-faced farmhouse and the milking parlour together with a large pond inhabited by frogs, ducks and moorhen. Behind this stood a tiny disused church which had once served the parish. Windy, often muddy lanes led to various fields, altogether covering some 240 acres. Despite being sold to my father, it continued to be run by the previous owners, the Hammerton family. Wheat, barley, oats and kale were grown on a rotation basis, together with root crops such as mangold, beet and potatoes. The livestock consisted of some thirty cows at the time of purchase, replaced in 1948 by beef cattle. Added to this were several Wessex saddle-back pigs and their litter, with three shire horses used primarily for their muscle-power – hauling logs about the place, trudging up and down the fields pulling plough, reaper or harrow behind them. Little need to go further. The 2012 BBC series *Wartime Farm*, filmed on the site, together with the accompanying publication[26], provide a vivid picture of life on the land at that time.

Father entered the new venture with great enthusiasm. The two gurus – Uncle Will and Mr Roberts – were consulted and there were constant trips to see how things were getting on. Brian remembered accompanying them on regular Sunday walks around the property with the manager, but Mother was not so keen, especially when it came to visiting other farms in the area to compare their progress with ours. Back home, Father joined the local *Farmers Club*, began reading up on the subject (A.J. Street became his favourite author) and listened to whatever was broadcast on the subject.

This included the weather forecasts. Initially these as were grim as they were accurate. Snow blanketed the countryside throughout the early weeks of January 1942, bringing much of the activity to a halt. Summer – when harvest is due – was always a difficult part of the year, especially as the land was heavy clay and not the easiest to work. There was little improvement in the weather, consequently the crops were almost ruined. The following year was no better, but 1944 was gloriously successful. The lifting of potatoes was no less worrying. Here, the perennial problem was wireworm which, if not caught in time, could devastate the crop. There was also the rumour that enemy agents had been distributing Colorado beetle with ruinous effect, while with fitting irony, prisoners of war from Germany and Italy were brought in to help out with the harvesting. They were completely

---

[26] Ginn et al, 2012

charming to everyone, especially us children, many of them remaining after the war to bring up families in the district. Probably the worst of all concerns was foot-and-mouth disease, which materialized in the epidemic of 1945.

To a five-year-old, regular visits to Botley Manor brought a whole set of new adventures. Assisting with the shelling of peas grown on one of the vast outfields was a welcome addition to helping out with Mother's jam or marmalade-making efforts, but the farm held even greater attractions. Joseph, the goat, for example, tethered among the tombstones in the churchyard, to ward off evil spirits. Or so the story went. Then there were the cattle, each with their own name, who'd wander unbidden down to the milking parlour once the gate was open in the evening, taking their correct places among the stalls. Here an individual member of the herd developed the unfortunate habit of kicking, so one of her back legs had to be tied up behind before milking began; next time she tried it she fell flat on her face. Meanwhile the shire horses, *Captain, Major, Colonel,* stood patiently back-to-back in the fields, facing in opposite directions, flicking flies out of one another's eyes with their tails. At the command "rats!" the farm dogs began a frenzied search, leaping around the barn and scratching among the sacks. I remember Father labouring all morning with the new churn only to produce 1 ¼ pounds of butter; bringing home our share of a pig under a government scheme; helping Mother prepare the braun. Brian, Dick, and occasionally Mary, had a splendid time driving the tractors and giving me rides. Most especially there were glorious weekends for all of us that summer, spent picnicking on the banks, boating, and swimming in the River Hamble.

Rats and rabbits together with smaller vermin, however, were a real problem; pheasants regarded as game. Brian's *Diana* air rifle was now replaced with a more deadly 4.10 shotgun. Too large and obviously too dangerous for a child to handle. Not so the *Diana*. Compact, lightweight and virtually noiseless. Simplicity itself. Natural, then, that by the age of eight or nine, I was only too eager to have a go myself. And was forbidden.

Inevitably, having taken careful note of how to load, take aim and fire, I'd wait till I was by myself, sneak it from the cupboard where it was kept, break it open, insert a pellet and set out in search of big game. Which turned out to be a small bird quite high up on the branch of a tree, singing its heart out. I set it in the sights, just like I'd seen the others do on their vermin- extermination missions, squeezed the trigger. There was a *thut!* a slight recoil, the singing stopped and the bird dropped from the tree. It lay, feathers ruffled by a slight breeze, claws clasped as if in prayer, silent at my feet. And I was responsible. For the life of me I don't know what I'd expected. Nor how to describe the horror I felt. Or what to do next. In the event I dug a hole, heaped the tiny body in it, covered it over, returned the gun to its cupboard, and have mentioned it to no one from that day to this.

By the beginning of 1944 the farm had been awarded First, Second and Third certificates of merit. The Hammerton family were still in charge, but Father had become what was known as a gentleman farmer. Whereas, he once told me, "I'm neither a gentleman nor a farmer".

RETROSPECTIVELY, IT'S THE previous year – 1943

– that can be seen as a turning-point in the war. Mother's diary records the steady retreat of the Germans from Russia throughout the early months, later the Allied advances in Tunisia; on 1st August the heaviest RAF bombing of Berlin, in September the invasion of Italy, leading through to D-Day and ultimate victory.

Throughout the conflict, Wickham had made a positive, if less direct contribution to the Allied success through a series of *Weapons Weeks,* aimed at raising money for the armed forces. Typical of these was the one, dedicated particularly to the Navy, which took place on 21 March 1942. Mother was on the platform for the march-past alongside the Australian Admiral Colvin, who took the salute. There was a church parade involving the Home Guard, a display of their weapons, a dance at the *Kings Head;* that evening a concert ("rotten" she declared). A large two-day auction was held in the square under the auspices of Messieurs Heyhoe and Page. The former was the north country fishmonger, having one of the loudest voices I've ever heard. I remember taking old newspapers across the road to him which he used for wrapping fish and chips. Mr Page was the village newsagent, barber, and bicycle repairer – a man of many parts. Altogether the auction made £600 towards the grand total of £1850.

A similar event, this time in support of the army, took place in November 1942. All of us were encouraged to look out any old books which when pulped could be used for the manufacture of military equipment. Badges were presented to children, promoting them from captain and up through the ranks according to the number of books they'd collected. Using a wheelbarrow I carted load after load down to the fire station, ending up as Field Marshal. Vandalism. God knows what went up in smoke as a result, but in a good cause. Two years later, in March 1944, Wickham celebrated *Salute the Soldier Week,* comprising a series of similar to those put on for the Navy, raising £85,000 nationally.

Otherwise, family life continued much as before: bike rides, jam making, family games, swimming at Hayling or Hill Head, regular trips to Gravel Hill, occasional forays north to visit Granny Bennett, Auntie May, a garrulous Uncle Albert and their daughter Dorothy. Brian and Dick were introduced to horse riding but did not take to it. Mary did, resulting in a broken arm.

And there were frequent visits to the cinema, followed by Mother's mini-critiques in the diary: *How Green is my Valley* ("very good"), *Gone with the Wind* ("fine, but too long and Reg did not like it"), *Young Mr Pitt* ("best film I've seen in years", according to Father), *The Ware Case* (she saw this five times), *Random Harvest, 49th Parallel, Clive of India* (all well received), and many others. I disgraced myself whilst at Preston by insisting on being taken to see a George Formby Film as a birthday treat when a trip to the seaside had been organized. Mary was detailed to escort me; sister/brother relations plummeting to nadir! 29th August was – however – a high point in family unity when she celebrated her twenty-first birthday at Gravel Hill. Later, on 17 September 1944, we gathered together to celebrate our parents' Silver Wedding Anniversary.

THROUGHOUT THOSE YEARS, Mother and Father had kept in relatively good health. As had the rest of the family. There had been the usual round of epidemics – measles, German measles, chickenpox, whooping cough, scarlet fever – common to anyone attending boarding school – together with minor infections, sniffles, sore throats, headache, indigestion, et cetera. Two cure-all medicaments would be applied to any and all of these. The first, obtainable from all chemists, was Dr Collis Browne's *Chlorodine*, a wonder cure, used by the family well into the 90s when its sale was prohibited. An essential ingredient, it turned out, was opium! The second panacea, concocted from Father's own recipe, consisted of a single measure (usually a spoonful) of set honey at the bottom of a tumbler, an additional two of whisky and twice the amount of boiling water. The potion was then stirred till all the ingredients were blended and drunk down as quickly as possible. A brew with which we were dosed regularly – myself from infancy – at the first sign of ill health. Fanciful maybe, yet it seemed to work miracles. As did another of Father's tipples: cold milk laced with soda water. At the time I thought this was his own concoction; whether he genuinely liked it, or took it for medicinal purposes. Either way, I'm glad the rest of us were not encouraged to do so. Turns out *dooka soda* is a nutritious beverage, popular in the Punjab, India and many parts of the East. As it became over here in Victorian times, when "bubble milk" became a nutritious pick-me-up with the introduction of cycling and for those involved in other strenuous activity.

On both fronts, at home and abroad, matters appeared to be going well. From the latter part of 1942 and over the next few years, though, a new, less happy, element runs Janus-like throughout the diary.

My parents had been kept extremely busy since the outbreak of war, but now the stress was beginning to tell. As well as Botley Manor Farm, Father had a business to run, together with the Monday stall at Fareham Market, the Home Guard, and weekly Masonic meetings. The hours were long, the responsibilities onerous and the family saw less and less of him. Mother was far from happy. He'd taken on too much, was tired and irritable; many evenings she was left completely to herself. She remembered how he'd been invalided out of the army in the previous war and now, for all his indomitable spirit, his energy began to flag. He was forced to take time off work and when he did, he was not the best of patients, refusing to take the rest he badly needed; always eager to get back to the office. Mother was just as busy, she was later to recall, looking after him, bringing up an energetic family, in addition to her work as billeting officer.

> As soon as I managed to find a home for any of those with me more came along, so quite a variety of children and adults were housed with me for varying lengths of time. During the day the various families were cooking, washing, bathing etc, and it was almost impossible to get into the bathroom in the morning or again at night then there was the continuous noise and shouting among the children.[27]

The situation was becoming acute and the doctor was called for – in those days he'd come to your home rather than vice versa – and advised her to take it easy. To facilitate this,

---

[27] Warwick, 1982, 26

the kitchen and scullery were brought up to date. Otherwise, bromide and nerve tonic were prescribed, which tasted vile so she refused to take them. Nor do either solution seem to have cut down in any way on her activities.

As always, Dr Kinnear was the physician in question. He was fairly young, ex-navy, direct of speech and brisk in manner. Mary would occasionally act as dispenser for him when qualified as a nurse. His mother, greatly respected throughout the village, had been at Cambridge with Miss Glenday, headmistress of Rookesbury Park School. Later I met the former on many occasions when organizing local WEA meetings, which she hosted at the Old House, where she lived with her son. I remember her dispensing tea from a Victorian caddy, mahogany with two glass jars – one for Indian, the other Chinese – having a silver spoon set into the lid for mixing. All tastes could be catered for according to proportion of each that were selected. Later in life I was to encountered Dr Kinnear as a patient on several occasions and discovered he did not suffer fools gladly. Once, having complained of a stomach upset, he gave me a rapid but efficient examination and told me to go away and dig the garden. I must have looked doubtful. "Expect something more spectacular?" he snapped. "A wonder cure; some miracle drug? When the simplest approach is often the best? Always has been. Read the story of Naaman in the Bible and be happy."

Turned out this was the powerful commander of a large army who suffered from leprosy. He was recommended to consult Elisha the prophet for a cure and went in pomp and ceremony only to be told to bathe in the Jordan seven times and he would be healed. The man was furious. An insult.

He'd expected great pomp and ceremony followed by a miracle cure; besides which this was a small, smelly river compared with those in his own country. "If the prophet had commanded you to do some great thing," they told him on return, "would you not have done it? How much more, then, when he says "wash and be clean?"[28] Good advice, and another example of the currency of Biblical narrative in daily life at that time.

Efficient though the doctor was, neither of my parents seemed inclined to do what he ordered. As far as their own health was concerned, that is, and – from this point onwards – hardly a member of the family escaped more serious illness.

The time had come for the next stage in brothers' education. Bloxham, just south of Banbury, seemed ideal and matters had been arranged for both boys to start there in September 1941. The beginning of each term was always anathema for Brian, despite having spent some years at the same school and doing well once he got there. Now, the thought of commencing again entirely from scratch was too much for him.

Knowing his love of the country, the notion of leaving Botley Manor farm behind might well have had a lot to do with it. Be this as it may, he made it through the first term, after which his anxieties began affecting his health more directly – agitation, jumpiness and nervous twitching. A specialist was called in, X-rays taken and it was advised he should take the whole of next term off. Granny came down from Preston and a bungalow – *Marina* at Hayling Island – rented

---

[28] See: 2 Kings V, 1—15

for three weeks in September. Father remained at Wickham looking after the business to which Mother returned as often as necessary to sort out billeting problems. Buses were infrequent and crowded so quite often she'd cycle as far as Havant, leaving the bicycle at the police station and catching the train to Hayling. There were a couple of bombing raids whilst we were there and the sound of distant gunfire, but the weather was glorious. All of us – Granny included – managed to swim and sunbathe on the beach.

No sooner had we returned when I went down with what must have been quite a serious case of measles, rambling incoherently according to Mother's diaries. Which was nothing compared with my sister's problems. In August 1943, whilst staying at Wickham she developed a temperature of 102 degrees, seemed to be on the mend, and was able to return to London on 2nd September. The illness returned in December and at 7am on 6th there was a phone call from the hospital saying she'd taken a turn for the worse. Mother hurried up to be with her, but Mary got no better. She was now suffering from pneumonia, the standard treatment being M & B (Sulphapyridine) tablets, and I remember the family's awe when the doctors decided to inject penicillin, the new miracle-cure. Before long she was in a wheelchair and by Christmas well on the mend.

Mother's workload continued much as before, whatever the doctor ordered. She was now Vice President, treasurer and assistant secretary of the Women's Institute as well as a district counsellor and billeting officer for the region. Her responsibilities might have become even more onerous had a proposal for Droxford RDC to amalgamate with Southwick come to anything. As it was, she now took on leadership of the local WVS (Women's Voluntary Service) as well as returning to her first love, teaching. This could have been at the Studio, maybe a space was found for such activities at Wentworth, but she soon had a small group meeting on a regular basis. All this as well as running a large house, the bringing up of two teenage boys and a somewhat troublesome child. My father's installation to a major position in the Masons on 7 October 1943, added to the burdens. The secrecy of the organization annoyed her. Whereas she was prepared to discuss her work on the council and listen to any advice he gave, Father was not permitted to reveal any aspect of what went on at his meetings. Worse still, they fundamentally disagreed on the quasi-religious aspect of the movement and would continue to do so for the rest of their lives. This despite his becoming Master of the Lodge in 1946.

All of which marks a clear change in the style, occasionally the content, of her diaries. Clearly she's overworked; tired, often irritated, occasionally depressed. The nadir seems to have been Easter 1943. Good Friday, she writes, has become "Bad Friday", followed by "Miserable Monday". A classic case of "burnout" we'd now call it, and little wonder. But it's herself she blames.

"What's wrong with me," she asks, "what's making me the way I am?"

Previous modifications to the kitchen area had not gone far enough, by October 1944, she'd decided the house itself was too large to run. *Preston Ridge* on Hoad's Hill, originally built to her own specifications in the pre-war years would, with the addition of two extra rooms at the cost of £1000, be far easier to manage. The Knight brothers drew up the plans and the family began preparations to move out of Wentworth.

Marking out the Square ready for troops and vehicles prior to D-Day, with Wentworth House behind (ivy-covered building, centre of row). The air raid shelter is the square brick building beyond the lorry, with SWS (Static Water Supply) alongside. (The Stan Woodford Collection, courtesy of Wickham Parish Council)

CHAPTER TEN

AFTERMATH

THE MOVE TO *Preston Ridge* never took place. Rather, the house was sold to the Blakes, quite possibly parents of the child involved with the tragic accident whilst an evacuee at Wentworth some three years earlier.[29] A team of seven men from Knights meanwhile began work converting Wentworth into a manageable family home. The whole of the rear wing was split off from the rest of the building. What had been the back staircase now led up to a single bedroom and bathroom, whilst permanent walls completed the division creating a fully independent flat. All achieved amid much disruption during the last week of 1944 and the first two of the new year.

Beyond Wentworth, momentous events were taking place. By now the Germans had been pushed right back to the Polish border and it became obvious that a second front would soon be opened. The centre for such planning was at Southwick, just over Portstown Hill, where Churchill, Eisenhower and the other wartime leaders frequently met. On one occasion the Prime Minister himself was scheduled to pass through the village. Crowds gathered on either side

---

[29] See Chapter Seven

of the square but no Winston Churchill appeared. They dispersed and Mother, crossing over to the shop, had to give way to a large black vehicle and a corpulent occupant who gave her friendly wave. And a "V" sign. Or so the story goes!

Wickham was abuzz with rumours. The push-back into Europe was eagerly anticipated, but no one knew exactly how or where it would take place. Mother's diaries provide a sad precursor – the death of General Powell who for so many years had led the Home Guard. On 4th March, six trees were planted in his honour following a memorial service at Shedfield church. On 15 March 1944, Mother saw thousands of planes streaming overhead; convoys continually passing through the village. Five days later travel within a ten-mile radius of the coast was banned whilst military vehicles of all kinds – trucks, jeeps, lorries, et cetera – lined up in readiness along roads around the village. For years afterwards fading yellow numbers could be seen painted onto walls indicating the positions assigned to each.

One of the Canadian soldiers, far from home, whiled away the time inscribing details of his regiment on the brickwork that separated Droxford Road from the Rooksbury estate. After the war, the District Council carved and blacked in the lettering as a permanent memorial of the occasion. Unfortunately, it was later destroyed, first by a falling tree, then – when replaced – in a road accident. Later in March 1944, all buses were requisitioned to transport troops to the coast whilst, ominously, coffins had been stacked up at Hall Court on the Botley Road for those who would never return. Then, on May 15, the whole square was taken up with fully loaded tank carriers. We watched countless numbers of them passing through the village in the early days of June till, on the 6th, D-Day was announced. That evening gliders streamed overhead as we listened continually for news on the radio. The diaries record the establishment of a bridgehead, the taking of Caen and of Cherbourg on 24th – the largest seaborne landing in history had begun.

A Canadian soldier inscribed details of his regiment and the date on a wall (courtesy of The News, Portsmouth)

But this was not a one-sided affair. Hitler now unleashed the first of his *Vergeltungswaffen* – "reprisal weapons". By now we had learnt to distinguish between all types of aircraft, both British and German, but on the night of 16th June came a sound none of us had heard before. A spasmodic, pulsating buzz, like that of a badly serviced motorbike. On the way down to the cellar we caught sight of an elongated cigar-shaped object in the sky; pilotless, with flames blasting continuously from its tail. Others were to follow, not planes at all but the V1s – enormous bombs – *doodle bugs* as they came to be known – propelled by a jet rather than the traditional engine attached above the fuselage. We came to dread the moment when, with a spluttering cough, the engine cut out and they plummeted to earth causing devastation wherever they fell. Not least frightening was the rudimentary navigation system, meaning that no one knew precisely where this would be.

Despite inaccuracies in the guidance systems, a large number of V1s got through to London. Mother visited Mary there later in the month and was appalled by the damage. Quite a few landed close to Wentworth, the whole house shuddering from the impact. The thought of the building collapsing, leaving the family buried beneath it, was too much for my parents. Besides which, Mother had continuously complained that the hours spent underground in the cellar was detrimental to our health. Knights were summoned to consider an air raid shelter in the garden. This would have been the Anderson type, providing a safe space one meter beneath the surface with corrugated steel panels bolted together, covered with a thick layer of soil and turf. Unfortunately, the earth proved too damp and we had to settle for the Morrison variation. Indoors it's true, but situated at ground level in the back wing of the house, consisting of a strong metal cage capable of withstanding any amount of rubble. Here we'd huddle when the siren sounded, clutching our torches and a battery-operated radio, waiting for rescue should Wentworth receive a direct hit.

Mother paid scant attention to the war after the D-Day landings. Bad news had reached her from Preston where her sister, Eva, was gravely ill with pleural pneumonia; followed by the news that on 11th she had died.

"There follows a mist and weeping rain/ And life is never the same again" Mother told the diary, quoting, misquoting rather, the poet George McDonald as she hurried north for the funeral. Her diary notes the continued advance of the Russians across the Rhine towards Berlin; the death of Hitler on 30th April, hostilities formally ending at 8pm with VE Day (8 May 1945). This was marked in Wickham with a service in the church. There was a huge bonfire in the Square with a live band playing music for dancing throughout the night. Other celebrations were to follow. 29th March the next year was designated Welcome Home Day, all the men returning from combat being presented with a tankard. Calculations as to the number required were incorrect so that fourteen extra had to be ordered. This was followed by a less success-ful Victory Day on 6th June. Sports, dancing, fireworks and a bonfire had all been planned, but it poured with rain and most of the activities had to be cancelled. There were yet further festivities on 15th August when the final victory over Japan (VJ Day) was announced.

The war might have ended but, despite the courage and comradeship, its aftermath was to be felt for many years to come. The village remained virtually unscathed, but Portsmouth and Southampton along with many cities throughout the country were scarred with bombsights and rubble. The large shelter erected opposite Wentworth stood for a decade or more, but individual Andersons came to be used for storage, garden sheds, kennels or play-dens for the children, whilst in many homes the now-redundant black-out proved a good source of material – the shorts in which

I played football for several years, for example. Meanwhile, silk-like parachutes provided more intimate garments for the ladies. It was almost a decade before rationing came an end whilst in May 1946, the government was forced to introduce a "Save Bread" campaign. Fuel was in particularly short supply, cars gradually appearing on the market; you could have any colour you wanted – so the story went – as long as it was black and were prepared to wait for a year or more …

Among those returning from the war were quite a few higher-ranking officers – admirals, colonels, commodores and the like – who were looking for retirement homes and fancied Wickham, nor was it long before they found their way into various levels of local government. Mother was not all that certain this was a good thing. Few of them knew much about the area and even those that did brought a certain style of leadership with them; one which, she felt, discouraged the participation of female candidates. Fortuitously for them, several large properties came onto the market, fallen into disrepair through loss of family members rather than direct bombing, their upkeep too high, and/or death duties proving their maintenance unmanageable. As with Botley Manor Farm, they would usually be put up for auction, the furniture and rest of their contents left in situ to be sold separately by individual lot. Mother was a great aficionado of such occasions, several pieces of furniture finding their way into Wentworth as a result. So, too, china teapots of all shapes and sizes that she had begun to collect. More intriguing were the boxes crammed full of odds and ends to be sold off as job lots. No matter how carefully one looked on the day Invariably there were surprise-finds at the bottom. These would be displayed for re-sale in a window she'd commandeered at the side of our shop across the Square.

If a number of the naval high-command were now surplus to requirement, so, too, were quite a few of our warships. Some were sold off abroad; others went to the scrapyard, but not before they'd been gutted of their equipment, furniture and fittings. Plaques and railings, rugs and chairs, clocks and compasses, pots, pans, and cutlery, often inscribed with the names of their ships, all were to be had in Portsmouth's second-hand shops. The largest of these was Fleming's, a splendid emporium on two floors which had narrowly escaped the bombing. We still have an ornate silver coffee service from one of the officers' messes presented as a Christmas of birthday present about this time. Undoubtably the most impressive of Mother's acquisitions, though, was the oak brass-strapped barrel emblazoned with the words *The King God Bless Him* in which the sailors' rum was stored. It remained in Wentworth until passed onto the next generation in 2018.

Peacetime brought a number of Mother's activities to an end. She continued helping with the clear-out of ARP equipment – helmets, shovels, sand-buckets, fire-extinguishers, etc – stored away in the Victory Hall. The WVS clothing-exchange scheme ran on for some time, but the bulk of her work with the evacuees was concluded. She decided to give up her seat on both District and Parochial councils, resigning from the former on 12 December 1946, the latter on 7 January 1947 having served for almost a decade on each. Depressing and fearful, she wrote, to have lived through those times, but:

it had its wonderful moments. There was so much kindness, comradeship and generosity shown by all. To me, this was Wickham at its best. Not even the terrible "Lord Haw Haw" with his nightly anti-British calls telling of disasters which eventually came to pass, could break the faith and the courage of the ordinary villager.[30]

At home there were regular sessions of jam-making, strawberry and raspberry for the main part, the new self-sealing Kilner jars with screw-down lids now taking much of the guesswork out of the proceedings. The orchestra had been resurrected and she continued her violin lessons. There was an expedition to Stratford for a performance of *The Tempest,* another to hear a speech by Aneurin Bevan on *Housing.* Nor had Mother's love of the cinema diminished. *Vanity Fair, Great Expectations, Lady Windermere's Fan, Nicholas Nickleby,* and *Great Expectations,* provide some evidence of her taste, but *Captain Kidd, Black Hussars, Bells of St Mary's* and *Spiral Staircase* can only have been to appease the children. The latter scared the living daylights out of me, but I adored all the *Tarzan* films starring the original Johnny Weismuller.

Brian, meanwhile, was to have one of his cherished hopes blighted. He'd left school at the end of 1944 to begin work with *Austin Wyatt's*[31], the land agents and auctioneers who ran Fareham Market. Together with Dick he'd been a keen member of the Bloxham YTC (Young Training Corps); now, still too young for conscription, he decided to volunteer

---

[30] Warwick, 1982, 24

[31] See Austin & Wyatt, 1987

for the Royal Navy. He was called up to London for interview, but did not meet their requirements. Father saw how depressed he was and took him to the Service's office in Portsmouth where they were advised he consider radar. This involved eight weeks of training, January and February 1945, in Skegness, but the old problem, nerves, returned and he was unsuccessful. However, he continued the course, which was very much to his liking, before returning to work at Austin Wyatt.

Brian, naval training, Scarborough, 1944

Mother and Father at a national conference, late 1940s

CHAPTER ELEVEN

BIRTHS, MARRIAGES, DEATHS

WITH THE WAR behind them the family optimistically saw in the New Year on 1ˢᵗ January, but 1946 had hardly begun when bad news arrived from Preston. Granny Bennett was desperately ill and Mother hurried north. She did what she could but soon needed to return to look after her own family and participate in various activities around the village. Here life continued more or less as before, yet the tone had been set for much of what followed. Added to the stress of running the business and the farm, Father now had meetings of the NFU (National Farmers' Union) and NFI (National Federation of Ironmongers) to attend, whilst the Masons remained a continual bone of contention. Grudgingly, Mother attended, even enjoyed, the occasional "Ladies Nights". And now there was the problem of the next stage in my education to consider.

It seems from the diaries that at the age of six I'd been put on a bus and sent to Wycombe House in Fareham. Thereafter I spent a short time at a tiny and very amateurish school run by a Dr Braham, at Newtown. My main achievement there was throwing an inkwell at one of the few other boys who were teasing me, leaving a stain on the wall. I failed the examination for Portsmouth Grammar; visits were made to several prospective schools in the area: Westbury House, West Hill, Sundal Manor, Storrington, Hurstpierpoint. Towards the close of the 1940s (and by now my poor parents must have been desperate) I ended up at two boarding schools. I don't recall much about either of them and the memories I do have are jumbled and not particularly happy ones (corporal punishment; public confessions of wrongdoing; a black book into which such beatings – administered by cane or table-tennis bat – were ritually recorded; pupils assigned a number for convivence [mine was 19]; brothers known as "Major", "Minor", "Minimus" – rather like the horses at Botley Manor Farm; a "pigs table" assigned to pupils failing the requisite niceties; and outside lavatories allocated for those not yet fully house trained).

Each of these schools proved unsuitable – either me for them, them for me, or both. It was beginning to look as if I was uneducable. None of this affected me directly, although it did seem strange the amount of money parents seemed willing to spend for the humiliation of their offspring.

Mary, by now fully recovered from pneumonia, had concluded her training and qualified as a state registered nurse on 9 June 1945. And she'd met John Donaldson, then a Lieutenant-Colonel in the army, serving in Germany. He proposed on the 21st and presented her with a single diamond ring. The engagement was announced in the *Times* and *Telegraph* and the wedding was set for 19th August as John was due to go to Burma. The posting, however, was cancelled, John was promoted, and the wedding set for 6th October. Disaster struck. The coupons we'd been saving up for her wedding dress were stolen but the villagers rallied round, pooling their own so she could be married in style. Panic also set in the night before the big day: her veil had gone missing, finally to be discovered behind a drawer. It turned out that the employee who'd stolen the coupons, and must have set all records for non-attendance, had been making off with small items from Wentworth. She was brought to justice and bound over for two years, about two-thirds of the loot being recovered.

The year, though, concluded with two happy events. On 31st August, Mother's niece Dorothy, named after her – tall, redheaded and splendidly outspoken – married Bill Threlfall. He was a mild, cheerful, asthmatic, delightful man. Then, on 3rd September, Mary gave birth to a 7lb 2oz baby girl. Michelle was the name John favoured and by which she is at first referred to in the diaries, within a few weeks, though, this was relegated to second-place following Margaret-Ann.

1947 began with atrocious weather conditions; the coldest for three centuries, apparently. The bitter chill of January soon turned to snow. Icy conditions made Portsdown Hill unpassable and on 1st February all bus services were cancelled. Coal stocks dwindled and eight days later electricity consumption was rationed to nineteen hours a day. There were blackouts, television was off the air, radio programmes were axed and newspapers reduced in size. Lucky Royal Family, Mother commented in her diary, off on tour to South Africa aboard *HMS Vanguard,* the last and fastest of battleship built during the war. She was later to be shown over the vessel, but found the experience disappointing. Road conditions remained perilous, on 29th February a car skidded in the village killing its two passengers and March brought further snowstorms. Then came the thaw and with it flooding, followed by almost continuous rain.

In the midst of all this Mother was once more called north where Granny Bennett was now desperately ill and not expected to live long. They had little time together before she died at 11:20 on 9th January. A service was held at Penwortham, but the funeral took place at Wickham in the bitterly cold on 13th. I'm not sure why this should have been but assume she wished to be buried alongside my grandfather who, so I believe, died on a visit south. The service was attended by a large contingent of the northern branch of the family, Mother returning with them on 21st to help sort out the furniture and Granny's belongings. There was a disagreement between Auntie May and Uncle Jack (Eva's widower) over who should have the sideboard, whilst Mother secretly coveted Grandfather Bennett's diamond ring, which was eventually given to Dorothy. The large regulator clock with my great grandfather's name on the dial did, however, came back with her to Wentworth, standing in the dining room for the next seventy years before being bequeathed to my brothers, eventually passing on to the next generation. It has now been in the family for around 170 years, a letter from Mother's sister – Auntie May – was later to trace its genesis:

Thomas Bennett ... originated from around Ormskirk where his father was a prosperous farmer, he naturally wanted to follow on. However, Thomas had ideas of his own and ran away from school and his home and apprenticed himself to a watchmaker in Preston. He was exceedingly clever and built the Regulator himself and got a cabinet-maker to make the beautiful case for the wonderful clock, which was unique at the time and still is, as mercury weights were then unheard of … He had four daughters and a son (Thomas) to carry on his name and all the family lived at 2 Lune Street over the shop … Thomas married at 21 and naturally joined his father on leaving school and on his marriage the business became "and son". All this time the regulator stood in the best position in the shop even after Thomas had acquired another shop at either side of his and knocked them into one main which formed the most important jewellers in the town … In 1926 he sold the business and bought 4 Cop Lane. The Regulator went with them of course and stood in the drawing room until Harriet (his wife) died. I well remember her last act before having to stay in bed was to come down in her dressing gown and wind it. I saw her pass her hands over it as though she knew that she was saying "goodbye" to it – as indeed she was.[32]

Back in the south, major renovations had been made to the Studio, converting it into a modern two-storey building, the upstairs section of the shop similarly converted into living accommodation. Snow and floods were followed by a glorious summer; Fair Day was more crowded than it had

---

[32] Mrs A. Collinson, to "Brian and Barbara" 11 July 1979

been for years and up at the farm the harvest went splendidly. We now had a beach hut at Hill Head, Brian and Dick cycled there or to Lee-on-Solent for a swim, and I was given a tent for my birthday. This was ex-army khaki, with just enough room for one adult stretched out in a sleeping-bag or two children providing they didn't stand up. It folded down into a neat bundle with pegs, guy ropes, articulated poles, etc tucked away in the centre – once the technique had been mastered, which it never quite was.

MOTHER HAD BEEN striving to cope with two deaths in the family, just eight months apart, when totally unexpected news arrived from Preston. Jack, Eva's widow had announced his engagement – eight months following her funeral. The name of the bride-to-be is not mentioned in the diary, nor did Mother attend the wedding on 19th July. All this coinciding with the third sister – May – entering the infirmary for a serious operation, the details of which are not disclosed. Once she'd recovered, and this took a long time, Mother and Auntie May hardly spoke of Jack again, and when they did it was always in a hushed, scandalized tone.

Their son, Stanley, was treated in similar fashion. A reasonably successful author, he published some twenty-five novels under his real name, S.B. Hough, as well as using the pseudonym Bennett Stanley, and Rex Gordon for science-fiction. The most successful by far was in the latter category: *No Man Friday*.[33] The source of Mother's displeasure, however,

---

[33] See: entry in *Encyclopedia of Science Fiction* eds John Clute and David Langford.

were occasional plots touching upon sex, violence and incest. Another of their sons, John, a Flight Lieutenant test pilot in the RAF was killed on 9 September 1953, whist piloting a helicopter at the Farnborough Air Show.

The weather remained hot, Mother turned out the box room, went to Hill Head for her first swim of the season, but on 24th July I witnessed a dreadful accident in the back garden. My brothers were playing golf, Brian took a swing of the club and caught Dick, who was standing just behind him, full in the face. He was rushed across to the surgery where Doctor Kinnear stitched him up. Had the blow been a little further to the left he might have been blinded; as it was the scars remained with him for life. That year he left Bloxham to conclude his studies at Portsmouth Municipal College.

As a celebration of the event, and no doubt help both boys forget the accident, Mother booked a holiday for them at Ventnor in the Isle of Wight. Diary entries for 28th and 29th August are left blank, before, on 30th came a final, totally unexpected entry:

"can write no more in my diary. Perhaps someday I may again but … not at present."

No explanation is given, although Mother had recently suffered the loss of those close to her. Life must also have seemed that much less interesting, the house emptier without the evacuees or various wartime projects to fill the days. Brian and Dick were contemplating their future, which – in all probability – meant they, too, would soon be leaving. Then there was the worry as to what was to be done about my own schooling, and little by way of recreation other than the orchestra and frequent visits to the cinema.

The 1939—47 diaries had come to an end, or so it seemed; for whatever reason, she genuinely appears to believe this was the case. But it proved to be no more than a pause. They mark the conclusion of probably the most eventful part of the story, but her career was not yet over. Nor by any means was she written-out. And, in one of many articles that were to follow, she summarizes sentiments often expressed when we were together:

> I suppose the inevitable had to come. One cannot stop progress, but changes seem to have arrived so suddenly. The quaint shopfronts have been replaced by modern shop fittings and large glass windows through which one can see at a glance what is being sold. All this has left his mark on Wickham. The square which used to be for the pleasure of us all has now become one huge car park, and one has to look up above the shining shop fronts to see the remains of the beauty of the older properties … It cannot be denied that modernising the village has made Wickham an excellent little business place, and that it could not for ever retain its old-world charm of the past. Something had to go. One cannot have the best of two worlds.[34]

---

[34] *Hampshire Chronicle,* 18 August 1978

R. G. WARWICK TRADING LTD.

Warwicks
of **Wickham**

Telephone:
01329 832531

WE HAVE WHAT YOU WANT - OR FIND IT

EPILOGUE

THROUGHOUT HER LIFE, Mother seems to have been driven by an impulse to write, and although the original diaries ceased in 1947, this compulsion reasserted itself just short of a decade later when once again she began recording daily events in and out of Wentworth. Father had died on 10 February 1956; Dick is married, with Brian soon to follow suite, whilst I am doing National Service in the RAF. Mother learns to drive, which seems to give her a new lease of life. Still no explanation for the silence though, no reference back to the nine hidden years; it reads just as if nothing had happened.

She returns to teaching in various capacities, is actively involved in a number of local activities connected with the elderly and the very young – notably as tutor to Portsmouth girls on the Nursery Nursing Certificate course – that is, when not helping out with the upbringing of the grandchildren – nine eventually, including Margaret-Ann, with her first great-grandchild arriving in 1974. She writes regularly for the local press – often under the pseudonym *Wickhamite,* her diaries continue through to 1978, one year short of her death, after which a number of bungalows for the elderly abutting the Square opposite Wentworth are named *Warwick Way* in her honour. Appropriately enough her tombstone at St Nicholas's Churchyard, Wickham, is inscribed with the words: *She Loved All Children.*

As for the rest of us, foundations laid in childhood can – with hindsight – be seen as having a large influence, if not determining, the paths we followed.

Mary was now set on a glittering nursing career that would lead her even further in the profession, later still to a prominent position in the field of politics, eventually as the first female Lord Mayor of London. Her husband John was to rise to one of the highest positions in the judiciary, as Master of the Rolls.

For as long as I can remember, my brothers were very different people: Brian the easy-going extrovert; Dick, thoughtful, resolute, the most practically minded of the lot of us. When Brian broke the wireless, it was Dick who mended it; when the handlebars of his cycle buckled, Dick made the repairs, and when the pellets for the airgun proved unsuitable, Dick came up with a solution. About the house, he mended the boiler when it broke down, constructed a table for family use, shades for our standard lamps and a hutch for the rabbits. After Granny died, the large regulator clock that had stood in her father's shop was passed down to Mother. It was damaged in transit, the all-important mercury spilling from its pendulum. Dick set to working out how to set things right, which he achieved after much experimentation.

Each of them was faced with important decisions towards the end of our father's life. Who should take over the running of the farm, who the management of the business, or should both enterprises go out of the family? Brian was an obvious choice as far as the former was concerned. He'd spent a lot of time at Botley, loved the place, but was aware of difficulties in the lay-out, the general unproductiveness of the clay soil, and declined. Following this he continued for a while with *Austin Wyatt*, after which his career progressed very much in the way one would have anticipated, working on the land in a number of capacities – among them the Coal Board and Hoveringham Gravel – eventually being appointed Estate Manager for Lord Derby.

Dick's decision went in the opposite direction. A course at Southampton University was discussed, but nothing came of this. Ahead lay conscription to the army. Having been a member of the Cadet Rifle team at Bloxham, he won the award of top recruit at Catterick Camp, and might have continued in a career where his talents could be applied to the full. However, it was becoming increasingly obvious that Father could no longer hold such a key role in the family business and Dick entered into partnership with him, later expanding the enterprise in a number of directions. One of his memorable innovations was the annual staff holiday abroad to places such as Sorento, Athens and Majorca largely subsidized by the firm. Throughout his life, he was to develop a number of interests – the cornet, ham radio, clock repairs, electronic organ – none of them set aside until they had been thoroughly mastered. But it was not till the very end that I discovered his brilliance at literary pastiche.

Amid all the activity, I turned out to be the quiet one – much more of a problem than either of my brothers. I got on well enough at home; who wouldn't in that part of the world with such a varied and resourceful family. Nor, when it came to it, did I have any objection to being sent away to school. It seemed the normal, accepted thing to do. Somehow though I just couldn't get the hang of it. Looking back, it always seemed to me as if such institutions were places designed to facilitate teacher-talk. What relevance such information had, or just what I was supposed to do with it was never explained, nor did this occur to me till in desperation my parents found Brickwall, a wonderful school situated on the Sussex/Kent border. Here, for the first time in my life, I met a group of teachers who treated me as an individual; actually seemed to enjoy their pupils' company. After which came national service in the RAF, London University and into a career in teaching (inspired by the notion that there must surely be a better way of doing things than I'd experienced). Eventually, after all the expense, worry and difficulties my backwardness must have cost, it might have been some recompense for Mother to see me installed as a university lecturer and to read my doctoral thesis. Had she lived just a little longer, she would have been even more delighted when I began supervising those of others. Amazed, possibly, when I became a professor. But not nearly as dumbfounded as I was!

The unsung hero of all our lives, though, must surely be Wentworth House. It has survived fire, flood, dereliction, ill health and explosives. Restored through an "ivory" renaissance in 1930, internal redecorations nine years later, a face-lift for the front façade in 1940 and the major renovation of 1944/5, it has in its time served as a school, a haven for the homeless, and – for three and half generations – the focus of family life for each one of us.

This is just as it had been in the early 1920s, recalled by ten-year-old A.V. Barber who spent several happy months at Wentworth:

Spring, summer, autumn and winter all have their different interests and excitements here in Wickham.

After the brown deadness of winter we love to see the first snowdrops in the garden. These are not lonely for any length of time but soon surrounded by the cheerful colours of the crocus. Then come walks in search of primroses and there is a new green everywhere. Easter is a happy time with the daffodils and chocolate eggs.

Summer means the smell of pinks and roses, going to the fair, picnics, and playing in the garden after tea.

Then summer fades into autumn and winter curtains go up.

We scuff through orange-coloured leaves and try to catch them as they flutter from branches. There is a smell of bonfire and we feel a little sad at all of the dying of summer.

Winter arrives with Jack Frost's lacy patterns on the window and the delicious crunch as we stamp on an iced puddle. There are parties: some with a magic lantern, and the shutters closed at teatime instead of the evening.

Just as it seems a world of dark and cold we are cheered by preparing for Christmas. We make paper chains and last-minute presents and are very busy with our secrets.

Carol singers knock at the door and wonderful smells reach from the kitchen. Nanny lets us eat the sugar off of the peel when she's preparing it for the Christmas cake.

And so the days go by taking their pattern from the seasons.

The old house shelters us and we love it.[35]

We live in the midst of change: work, fashion, values, leisure, entertainment, technology; these days everything seems in a permanent state of flux. Basically, though, the family as a unit and the way they occupy our time seems to have remained much the same. So, too, Wentworth. Current conversions mean it faces a new future, providing opportunities for a number of entrepreneurial or social enterprises in the years to come; yet wholly appropriate given the background and nature of the Warwick clan.

---

[35] Barber, 1966, 63

BIBLIOGRAPHY

Anon, *A History of Austin & Wyatt, 1836—1986,* 1987.

Barber, A.V., *Days at Wickham,* London, Geoffrey Bles, 1966.

Barker, Brown & Greer, Horndean, *The Cinemas of Portsmouth,* 1981, 0 903852 15

Doughty, M., (Ed), *Hampshire and D-Day.,* Crediton, 1994, 1 85741 047 5

Ginn, Goodman & Langlands, *Wartime Farm,* London, Mitchell Beazley, 2012.

Kraemer-Johnson & Bishop, *Southdown Memories,* Hersham, Ian Allen, 2009,

Montgomery, A., *Tom, Tom, the Farmer's Son,* Portchester, Alan Montgomery, 1987, 0 9512261 0 X

O'Connell, Leatherhead, *Southwick, The D-Day Village that Went to War,* Ashford Buchan & Enright, 1994, 1   85253 299 8

O'Donald Mays, James, *Sweet Magnolias & English Lavendar,* Burley, 2008, 978 0 907956 07 5

Preston, E & Wallis, S, Tiverton, Halsgrove, *The Forest of Bere,* 2006, 1 84114 516 5

Stone, R.A., Southampton, Kingfisher, *The Meon Valley Railway,* 1983, 0 496184 04 6

Tappenden, B., *A History of Wickham,* Wickham, 1996, 0 09528994 0 X

Warwick, D.A., *Meon Valley Memories,* Farnham, Ricktomes, 1982, 0 9508328 0 4

Warwick, D.A., *Bygone Wickham,* Farnham, Ricktomes, 1983, 0 9508328 1 2

Warwick , D., "The Folk History of a Doomed Landscape", Salisbury, *Hatcher Review,* 1993, 5.35, pp 3—15

Warwick, D., *Chorus Endings,* Leicester, Troubadour, 2016, 978 1785892 035

Whinney, R., *Wickham Place, Excavation & Research, 1975-80,* Winchester, 0 86135 007 3

Wickham History Society, *Images of Wickham,* 2020

Wickham History Society, *Guide to Historic Wickham,* 2018

ACKNOWLEDGEMENTS

HOME FRONT WICKHAM could not have been written without the encouragement, help and advice of a wide range of people to whom I owe a large debt of gratitude.

Firstly, my wife, Ann, for her continual patience and encouragement, and sister-in-law Barbara who has been steadfast in her support since the project began.

My nephew John also, for his invaluable assistance with the Warwick photo archive. Acting on the side of caution, he was also my doppelganger throughout, sharing all text and correspondence with the publishers. Nor would I wish to neglect the rest of the family, far too numerous to mention by name but all of whom have contributed in one way or another over the years.

Specialist advice was provided by Dr Gareth Edwards of the *Portsmouth History Centre* and genealogical research by Sam Davenport. Geoff Phillpott of the *Wickham History Society* (https://www.wickhamhistory.org.uk) was generous in his help with the village photographs, and David Jump with technical assistance relating to the text.

Every effort has been made to trace and credit all copyright holders. Please accept my apologies for any errors or omissions. Corrections and amendments will be gratefully received and included in future editions of this book.

Finally, and by no means least, to Lorna Brookes not only as editor but for the enthusiasm, experience and expertise she brought to the project, and the care she and her colleagues at Crumps Barn Studio took in seeing it through to conclusion.

ABOUT THE AUTHOR

DAVID WARWICK is a retired university lecturer from Hampshire.

Following his National Service in RAF Fighter Command, he studied History and Theology at the College of St Mark and St John, London University. He has served as a teacher, senior lecturer and professor at schools and universities across the UK and abroad.

He has written widely in fields of Education, Management and Religion, including *Team Teaching (Hodder & Stoughton), The Modular Curriculum (Blackwell)* and *The Wealth of the Nation (Nicholas Brearley).* He served as indexer for Whitaker's Almanack for many years.

David is married with two adult sons and two grandchildren, and he and his wife Ann have recently celebrated their Diamond Wedding Anniversary.

If you loved this book, you'll love these
other history titles ...

HAROLD AND JOAN, LETTERS HOME
Harold Butler, edited by Karen Geraldine Croft

A tender and revealing collection of letters written by Harold
Butler to his wife Joan while training in Edinburgh as an army
driver, and then on manoeuvres in North Africa. Shares the life
and domestic cares of a soldier and his family during WWII

ISBN 9781915067180

THE STORY OF
BURY ST EDMUNDS MARKET CROSS:
the history, the actors, and the architect Robert Adam
Adrian Tindall

The Bury St Edmunds Market Cross was designed in 1774 by
the celebrated architect Robert Adam. This 'neat and beautiful
theatre' is a brilliant example of decorative neoclassical
architecture. But beneath its feet lies an older story. Marking
250 years since Robert Adam first revealed his design,
archaeologist Adrian Tindall tells the story of this iconic
landmark and the people who created it

ISBN 9781915067432

Crumps Barn Studio
www.crumpsbarn.online